Thomas Gordon Hake

The Serpent Play

A Divine Pastoral

Thomas Gordon Hake

The Serpent Play
A Divine Pastoral

ISBN/EAN: 9783337779689

Printed in Europe, USA, Canada, Australia, Japan

Cover: Foto ©Lupo / pixelio.de

More available books at **www.hansebooks.com**

THE SERPENT PLAY

A DIVINE PASTORAL

BY

THOMAS GORDON HAKE

London
CHATTO & WINDUS, PICCADILLY
1883

THE SERPENT PLAY

B

DRAMATIS PERSONÆ.

HUMAN CHARACTERS.

CŒLIS, *the Soul-Seeker*.
VORAGINE, *a Warrior*.
VIVIA, *the Sister of Cœlis*.
VOLUPSA, *the Sister of Voragine*.
HAYUS, *a Priest of Kausis*.
Messenger.

DIVINE CHARACTERS.

PSYCHE, *the Soul*.
KAUSIS, *the Destroyer*.

OTHER PERSONS.

PANDOLPH, *the Brother of Cœlis*.
BEATRICE, *the Wife of Pandolph*.
Actors.
Spectators.

SCENE: *The Ophidian Hills*

ACT I.

PROSCENIUM.—*The Gates which lead to the Paradise of Cœlis.*

CŒLIS, Messenger.

MESSENGER.

Scarce need you private tidings, for the war
Is its own chronicler : the Ophidian streams
Are thick with blood, here clinging to the bank
In clots like the red fungus, there in floods
Down-bearing through the gulleys to the town
Its grim advices. In the spattered dust
Lie stretched the fallen corpses of the foe
Like a hewn forest. Rampant victory
Appals the leaders, and the priests have fled
Their sanctuary. Hayus only stays
To meet us with unhoped for terms of peace.
His foresight, keen as vision, has o'erruled
The councils: they accept the conquering Cross
That roots out Serpent-worship from the world.

CŒLIS.

A sanguinary peace then ends the war.
Would I had gone to learn the people's wants ;
To yield them even more than they desired :
Then had they risen higher than their creed,
Now their sole refuge.

MESSENGER.

So it might have been,
Had you first striven to cleanse the common faith
Of its idolatry. In days scarce gone
Well we remember how our villagers
Obeyed your word, at which the worship dropped.
But little trust in friends have jealous foes :
They know we have already doomed their creed
In setting ours aside.

CŒLIS.

Why is it crushed
When by example 'twas so sure to fall?
Our aims are now degraded, 'tis too late
To remedy the wrong : yet from this time
May Voragine show mercy to their souls,
Not flash the Cross before them to impose
Belief that adds new torture to their wounds.
Say this from me.

MESSENGER.

I only can obey.

THE SERPENT PLAY.

CŒLIS, *alone.*

Be ever distant from this blessèd seat
His ruthless bloodhounds, Conquest and Defeat !
Can these, that even the reptile rite debase,
An old religion by a new replace ?
Alas ! if one so must the other fall,
For what is new is never natural.
In this contented home our people find
The lull of peace; not so my shaken mind !
But shall I murmur when so many cares
In nature's uncomplaining heart abide ?
These horrors on her fall, and she forbears !
She chides not ; she has none to chide.
Yet may we see a shudder underlie
Her smile, that masks no base hypocrisy
But inner depths of goodness so conceals
That ages must elapse ere she herself reveals.
We worshipped her in every tree that grew,
Once deemed each rustling leaf her secret knew :
The juicy fruits, to golden goblets swelled,
Which to our lips the stooping branches held,
We deemèd her conscious gift. But time outwore
The freshness that her new creation bore ;
And thought sank deeper into things outside,
While they themselves sublimely deified.
God journeyed onward like a mighty wind,
But left the Soul that governs all behind,
Even from the sun-flame to the tended flower
That dies not out, though lasting but an hour.

Scene I. — *The Paradise of Cœlis among the Ophidian Hills.*

Cœlis, *a'one.*

CŒLIS.

' Here, like a quiet child, while Summer plays
Around the dwelling, as in earlier days,
Purpling the vineyards, sparkling on the rills;
Gliding from flower to flower, till overflows
The perfume-breath of the full-bosomed rose,
I hail my paradise, my native hills!
Here am I still; here my lost sires repose
Under the mortal ban, that, ere their birth,
Blighted the future of this alien earth,
And in death-twilight bade their senses close.
Weak was the will that in a guardless hour
Was shackled by the Serpent's power!
Shall not some soul his subtle chain unbind
And live for ever as at first designed?
Not by the ways that sorcerous spirits choose!
But who can find the true one? The recluse
Sees promised lands beyond the grave:
He listens for the angels' voices
That say the mystic Cross shall save,
And with clasped hands he, to the last, rejoices.
Some gather in a crucible of clay
The herbs that hold earth's throeful sweat,

With them to quench the thirst of their decay,
And to acquit themselves of nature's debt.
But from earth's essence who shall souls renew,
Or from its flowers the life-elixir brew?
O Love, thou only way! My spirit sate
With gazing through thee: then shall it arise
To visions of a heavenly paradise,
And with them reach what seem the empty skies!
The Sun, my flaming sword, is at the gate
And waves the way I seek.'

    His fathers' grave
Lay nigh, yet there the more to life he clave,
New meanings catching up from olden lore.
'The Serpent broke man's will of yore,'
He cries, 'and now the soul bemoans its realm
Long passed away, death left, to overwhelm
The thought that dares lost hope explore.'
He looks up towards the height; there stands
His castle o'er the triple-circling road.
He muses on his legend-haunted lands:
These were the ancient Snake's abode
In days of old romance, as told the bards;
And every gate even now the Serpent guards,
As, coiled upon a golden field,
For ages it hath lain across his father's shield.
He thinks how once a leafy parasite
It clomb the trees and with a reptile's might
Strangled their trunks, the forests all enthralling,
Till foe to man upon its belly crawling.

His steps now pause before a brook :
'Twas but the waters o'er the pebbles shook,
Yet seemed they spirit-voices meeting,
And nature's gossip-lore repeating.
One shrilly said : 'Look up and see.'
One murmured low : 'The apple-tree.'
The first then babbled : 'It is blazing
With ruddy fruits.'
The other said : 'It burns and shoots,
And eyes are gazing.'
And then another : 'Have a fear,
The Snake is here.'
Then murmurs reach him through the bracken,
Of air-gusts that delight to teaze,
While fern-plumes in their stately silence shaken
Wave to and fro in concert with the breeze.
He listens as to woman's voice they listen
Who watch to see her beauty glisten
While her voice murmurs : so he yields to sleep,
Charmed by the sights and sounds that o'er him sweep.
Sultry, the air for lofty life is burning ;
He dozes on, his thoughts returning ;
Into green spires of flame the fern-stems leap ;
Balls of hot fire the glowing apples seem :
He dares not wonder, lest his dream
Should vanish and flash down the naked stream.
The fern-flames speak with tongues that never tame,
The apples burn and utter silent flame.
The brook swells higher ; hissings fierce
Through its frothy torrent pierce.

Then comes a vision of the ancient Snake,
Even as one sees by day when wide-awake ;
Its head is rolling in the fern,
Its coils are round the boughs where the red apples burn.

Then the Snake whispers, and voices are hushed ;
Into its accents the silence has rushed ;
Crisp is the roll of its tongue and intense
Are the glozings it pours on voluptuous sense.
And still 'tis in whisper that seemeth to say :
'Thy moments are weary, prolong not thy day ;
Thy life-time is weary, prolong not the chase
After days without ending ; from all they recede ;
Of all mortals alike is fantastic the creed ;
Who hope and who mock end alike in the race.
Seize on rapture while yet it is nigh ; a new mortal,
Thou enterest the world through a glorious portal,
All riches to scatter, all homage possess :
Seize on love without stint and all beauty caress.'

On this the dreamer sees a phantom throng
Of rosy maidens float along ;
Towards him they droop their wavy arms,
Alluring him with lagging charms ;
And ever with a fonder face
Comes on new beauty with its newer grace.
O frantic pleasures, soul-dissolving !
O passion that once felt endures,
And bliss for evermore assures !

The brightest stars in heaven decline,
But joys about the heart revolving
With it ascend and still their own past light out-
    shine !

SCENE II.— *The Temple of the Serpent Kausis, in
the Paradise of Cœlis.*

CŒLIS, *alone.*

CŒLIS.

' Is sleep a darkness when my inner sight
Fills spaces where dissolving worlds belonged?
New visions, soul-enchanted, thronged
Around me in the vanished light !
Whence came they but from this creative will?
Then may it not the empty regions fill
With shapes more lasting from its own recesses,
When thus a living light the soul possesses?
But where shall this, my dream-creation be?
The sun-realms teem with works of One alone ;
She thinks and all is real ! She can see
The things Her soul hath imaged forth and done.
In virgin generation she conceives,
And to the expanding range her boundless nature
    gives.
Still the Snake rules below ! With fated power
He filched from man all time, all save an hour :

How soon run out! Is it indeed too late
To plead the heirship to that lost estate?'

The snaky pillars of the temple hide
Among the leaves at the brookside;
None now, save Cœlis, ever dare
To breathe the false, infectious air.
Within, a serpent-idol hangs
With hideous coil and poison-dripping fangs ;
And hissings as from hollow caves below
Enter the breezes, blowing where they blow,
And many a wayfarer affright
Who ventures thither by the pathless night.
Since Cœlis bade the Serpent-worship end,
For the Ophidian rites would none contend ;
Still, unseen spirits round the temple rage
And bring to earth again a darker age.
There are the graves, and there the days gone by
Flit round them, memory on memory ;
There thick as matted cobwebs lie
The souls of priestly warriors at rest,
And every knoll in consciousness invest.
Cœlis looks up the sloping grass
Where locust-trees in leafy shade bestride
The ancient path on either side,
And flutter o'er the sward while high the breezes
    pass.
He sees slow-crumbling through the boughs
The fane that holds his fathers' vows,

Where now the weird, unhallowed noises
Change into imploring voices,
That hymn the cabalistic prayer,
Poured from the writings on the walls engraved ;
That ever speak though none be there :
Even as survive the old-world memories
That writ in fire by the Prime-mover
Break out upon the phosphorescent seas
And turn, like scrolls, their glowing pages over.
O records worthy to be saved !

   The wind is now upon the shivered rills ;
Soughing sounds creep o'er the hollows ;
A twilight film hangs o'er the hills
And through its shrouds the shadow follows.
To the low breeze the anthemed voices come
And whirl about their holy home.
The spirits of the dead are singing,
Down the darkened glacis bringing
The tongueless prayers that through the walls are
   ringing.

ANTHEM OF THE DEAD.

'O Spirit, self-burning !
Soul of Decay !
Summer adjourning
In wintry array,
That ever returning
Thou sweepest away !

Leave us the fruit-time ;
Leave us the root-time ;
Winter is long !
Leave us the corn-time, leave us the grass-time,
Thou art the Strong !
Let the old sluices
Run down with the juices
Of olive and vine :
The oil flows from thee and thy blood is the wine.
Then shall we drink through thy wintery pastime
And shout o'er the wiles that thy wisdom instils,
And the good out of ill that thy cunning fulfils :
Shout to the hour when our breath we surrender
To thee our loved Spirit, our Lord, our Defender.'

    Trembling but bold, he mounts the stair,
When all is hushed : he cannot hear
A breath, so deep appears the lull of prayer.
Then he essays to draw the bar
When seems a thunder-bolt to grate afar ;
The unlocked heaven is shuddering for war.
And now, the winds through cloud-realms vaulting
    higher,
The thunder throbs pierced by the forkèd fire,
And sky-lakes plunge down heights sublime,
On the world's waters beating hurried time.
Yet in the rivers through the thunder pouring
And in the rushing wind-tides ever roaring,

To his strong soul one harmony abounds.
The several storms that rage, in concert play,
While the wide-engulphing sounds
Hold the racked hills and valleys in dismay.
And he is less alone on earth !
For lonely is the man whose spirit is
In concert only with eternal bliss,
And clashes with the concert of world-mirth.

Scene III.—*The Hall of Voragine.*

Volupsa *and* Cœlis.

Is he not lone when none his cares partake,
And woman would his faith in nature shake ?
Yet there was one he loved, and ever sought
When hope's excesses their own misery wrought.
Volupsa from the early day
Whereof the memory was childish play,
Had kept his heart as 'neath a vow :
But his meek love is humbled now ;
To him it seems but as a summer rose
That bloomed, then dropped where the sweetbriar
    grows.

CŒLIS.

Volupsa ! Life with us is lonely ;
All day you speak to few but me,

And I, with hundreds near, can only
Yourself with eyes of pleasure see.

VOLUPSA.

But, Cœlis, soon we both shall welcome others :
Your darling sister Vivia and our brothers !
We shall be blithe for many a day
And laugh o'er all the absent voices say !
The more that length of waiting makes us weary,
The more will every heart be cheery :
Those whom we love are on their homeward way.
We need no other pleasure seek
Than to look on towards days so surely pending :
Time may creep slowly, yet has many a week
One happy morrow for its ending.

CŒLIS.

Your brother ! Tell me his return is sure :
No other morrow shall my heart implore
Than that of peace. But time, I fear, effaces
In my young brother's breast the love of home :
New life in him wears out the early traces ;
Here all is old ; he will not come ;
Not even when to his princess wed,—
Unless it hap we all are dead !

VOLUPSA.

His absence is but of a year :
Sooner than you surmise he will appear.

CŒLIS.

No, he must stay in foreign courts
And there enjoy the savage sports;
Hunt the scared fox, run down the boar,
Stalk the red deer, pursue the roe,
And chase the plunging buffalo,
With times of hawking kept in store.

VOLUPSA.

Not strange it is to see a comely youth
Pursue his pleasures with the lords,—
Though strong may be the contrast it affords
To your pursuits of hidden truth.
Dear Cœlis, better were it far
That you had followed in the raging war
With my brave brother Voragine,
Who has so many battles seen!
Better than to be lost in fruitless musing!
Eyes pierce not nature and the heart
In her high symphony has little part :
Thought there but gambles and is ever losing.

CŒLIS.

Had I his tastes I could be wise :
I go but as the arrow flies.
Who shapes the bow the arrow shapes,
And none for long his doom escapes.

VOLUPSA.

Whence come these sayings sad and wild?
You were so cheerful when a child!
Too short for us was then the day,
And only tired-out eyes put off our play.
Now with a startling earnestness you meet
The same light hours half-way.

CŒLIS.

Can we repeat
Our infancy? Did we not then rehearse
With upstart zest our youth, our later age,
Before they came, and, on our little stage,
In arbitrary games all things reverse?
There lay our life, and only there
Can we look back devoid of care.
The times at last are true: the latest cry
Is war and Voragine's sage strategy:
How he the unsuspecting foe decoys;
How he their crops at harvest season,—
Their very towns with greedy fire destroys.
He makes men's lives the penalty of treason!
It is a feverish tale.

VOLUPSA.

He but performs
His duty when their fortresses he storms.
Despite these deeds is he not kind?
There never was a truer mind.

CŒLIS.

Brave though he be, and fearing not to die,
Where is the pride of his humanity?
To him the higher life is lost
Who honour gains at honour's cost.
Look at our people, how their fields are teeming
With plenty for the year's supply!
The harvest-moon is nightly beaming
With gratulations of the Deity.

VOLUPSA.

Yes; it is sad; but how can we evade
The woes whereof this world is made!
Even you at last to this dark war assented.

CŒLIS.

And from that hour to this have I repented.
Even better had it been to share the fate
Of those who hope though they but death await:
Blessed are the souls who, early though they die,
Have striven to touch the highest destiny.

SCENE IV.—*The Harvest-plains outside the Paradise of Cœlis. Night.*

CŒLIS, *alone.*

CŒLIS.

The moon is at the full and overflows;
The wheat is gathered into sheaves,
And heaven its quiet brilliance throws
On reapers who from toil repose
On the warm ground with flocks and beeves.
They, tired of grazing; tired of reaping;
O'er all the harvest-moon is sleeping;
All in illumined slumber bask and I
Alone keep the Eternal company.
The reapers lie full length, their hooks at hand;
The shepherds, at their midnight ease,
Their heads have pillowed on their knees:
Time moves not, sharing in their peace
And loitering on the yellow land.
A spell is upon all, the vultures sleep
Above in rocky nests, the wolves are charmed,
None fear the others, none the vigil keep,
But undefended here they sleep unharmed.
O friendly tomb! whence with re-opening eyes
These dreamy dead shall on the morrow rise!

ACT II.

PROSCENIUM.—*The Gates which lead to the Paradise of Cœlis.*

CŒLIS, Messenger.

MESSENGER.

I bear the words of Voragine.

CŒLIS.

Begin :
Erewhile his words were still the battle's din.

MESSENGER.

The vulgar cry for liberty is lulled;
Bright is the sword again that blood had dulled :
As though it flashed the miracle of peace,
'Tis only lifted now and murmurs cease.

CŒLIS.

In terror sown, the seeds of hate
Take easy root and germinate :

So, for our foes a better time is near,
And their revenge it is our turn to bear.

MESSENGER.

Their homes laid out in desert, who shall know
A seed-time where but weeds henceforward grow?
The earth is charred; priests, chieftains, all have fled
Into the burning forests and are dead.

CŒLIS.

Nature herself not spared ! yet ere the year
Will she revolt and her new weapon wear :
On the burnt soil will man again appear.

MESSENGER.

Who looks so far?

CŒLIS.

Not Voragine, 'tis clear.

MESSENGER.

But many a day beyond his morrow
Is safe ; at glorious spring-time, which is near,
The chief returns ;—

CŒLIS.

With him our reign of Sorrow.

CŒLIS, *alone.*

Can Nature sanction this, even war espouse
Wasting the scanty moments she allows,

Lest the religion to her trust reposed
Be to our precious leisure here disclosed?
The seer may vainly seek for holy soil
Whose sod the wily sorcerer turns over,
Though but to bare a serpent's coil
Or some more warlike creed discover.
But faith suffices with the sword's defence,
And sets aside the cruel evidence
Death's face affords, a warning all believe
And sicken at; unwilling to receive.
Thus must the disaffected soul resume,
In its resolve eternally to live,
Some war of vain desires whose creed shall vanquish
    doom.
I, too, will struggle through all hope, though none
The immortal life, since life first was, hath won.

Scene I.—*The Paradise of Cœlis.*

Cœlis, *alone.*

CŒLIS.

' Summer and winter changing hands
The green leaves hang mid red and yellow;
The fruits are over-ripe and mellow;
Cracked to the core their germ expands
And hope is heir to nature's sway,
Though now embowelled in decay.

Even while they vanish, Nature drapes
In her autumnal pride their lovely shapes.
Beyond the forest's brink pale clouds
Float o'er the foliage to take up its blaze,
While the sun glittering through the woods
Steeps their last beauty in his slumbering rays.
But he that set the stamp of death on man
At the fate-haunted tree still guards the portal
To thwart my soul that would escape the ban
And upon earth recover days immortal.
Nature's High Fast begins : life's latter stage
Glows in the ruddiness of age ;
Then, as the pomp of dying holds the scene
In slow procession, proud that it has been,
All drops ; the wondrous death its heritage.
So we approach the end ; o'er sodden leaves
The naked boughs stretch forth their dripping eaves,
Sapless and dark ; their potent virtue spent
Whose leaf-dome was the world's green firmament.
The skies are humbled in their grey attire,
And from the tree of life the fruit is gone ;
The flowers no more put forth their meek desire :
All things, one with another ; yet alone !

'She is eternal,' so all being cries,
'Whose hope this wreck of summer underlies;
Still is the scene mortality ! The day
That comes is not the one that passed away ;
The summer festival, so late outspread,

Was new as though no other had been kept;
But hope has not among its remnants slept,
And hope is older than the dead.
The life I seek while this brief being wanes
She gives me; she this deathless hope sustains;
She is the Soul of All; she permeates
Winter and spring, and, nowhere wholly hidden,
In me these restless watchings undertakes:
I seek her not unbidden.'

    In death new changes still arise;
The air hangs thick upon his paradise;
The brook-waves lie in waves of ice.
Where is now the flight of graces,
Sighing bosoms, happy faces,
Hands beckoning to some exalted goal
Which, never reached, with rapture filled his soul?
Volupsa, is her human charm forgot?
In this deep hour of love it flashes not!
A dream translates his self-exalted sense
Into the phrenzy of omnipotence.

'But,' cries he, 'dreams that come to pass are true:
Through them, the early messengers of doom
Forewarn us, ere the day is due,
Though they abide their time in the maturing
    womb.
Those spirit forms I saw; though they elude
My touch they come and live within my sight:
On their fond images I brood
Now as a future, now a past delight.

As they return to me, uncalled, I gain
Assurance of a life for ever real,
That he shall covet not in vain
Who seeks it once through his beloved ideal.
But when shall my slow-filling vision see
  The one, O Soul! whose likeness is of Thee?
When, gazing in the mirror of her love,
Shall I, beyond it, find the one above,
Who holds this grave of nature that the dead
Awake once more in summer garmented?
Reveal thyself, O Psyche, soul supreme,
With whom these calm and awful systems teem!
If, through long seeking, I thy love may claim,
Divulge to me thy most mysterious name,
That by these lips the one ecstatic word,
Be spoken, and to Thee again outpoured.'

  Then answers him the Soul of All;
The name is on his ears descending,
In strains that surely towards him fall,
And end in inward harmonies unending.
Her name as from a holy choir is springing;
He overhears the distant minstrelsy,
That seems as of departing spirits singing,
But leaves his frame in ecstasy to be;
Bliss chiselled from eternal harmony.

Scene II.—*The Forest.*

Volupsa, *alone.*

VOLUPSA.

I.

When I think of thee, brother,
    Is my heart not all thine?
Yet the face of another
    Seems bending o'er mine.
I call thee by name, yet a name not thy own
Has whispered already its dear undertone.

II.

When I think thine eyes greet me,
    Their sweet flash of blue
Brings another's to meet me
    Of somberer hue,
And ever before me they seem to remain,
Though my heart but repines to behold thee again.

III.

When I list, and would hear thee
    Once more in our home,
And thy voice appears near me,
    Another's has come.
I dream of thee only, for thee only sigh,
Yet thy image forsakes me; another's is nigh.

IV.

When thy fond smiles come o'er me
    As in moments now flown,
There riseth before me
    A look not thy own :
'Tis thee I recall to my mind, O my brother !
Yet ever with thine comes the gaze of another.

CŒLIS, VOLUPSA.

Volupsa knows the wanderer's haunt and strays
By paths wherein she feels his heart has spoken ;
And though the spell to her remain unbroken,
Not less the depth of silence may betoken
A love that but its voice delays.
No match was she, pure, simple-hearted maid,
For one whose soul must soar and cannot wade :
So when they meet, she only thinks how high
The hawk ascends through its blue hunting fields
In search of prey it finds not in the sky,
But in the hedges where the sparrow builds.
Then would she hold him in the gaze
She lifts to heaven when she prays,
And say, O Cœlis ! wander here no more !
Magic arts you disavow,
Yet at false shrines you surely bow,
And spirits of the unknown world adore ;
Agents of ill who would our souls decoy ;
Who dark, alchemic arts employ,

And false to seeming true transmute,
Beyond the reach of reason to refute.

CŒLIS.

Is life, then, dear one, such a pleasant travel
That what is next 'twere best not to unravel,
But shut our senses lest they knowledge find
Of marvels in advance and wonders left behind?
Our fathers so let slip their will and died.

VOLUPSA.

What we resign to heaven, is sanctified.

CŒLIS.

When you speak thus all doubtful things seem true;
They take your beauty and resemble you;
Then is my boasted will of poor account.

VOLUPSA.

Into the airless void it strives to mount:
Here is it unrestrained; this pleasant throne,
Older than many kingdoms, is your own:
Suffices not a power so great? But more,—
In seats of learning where the youth dispute
None could your subtle arguments confute.
But there are wonders fruitless to explore.
What can the meaning be of secret lore
But that all things remote are hidden,
And to the scrutiny of all forbidden?

CŒLIS.

It is not man invents desire,
And what he craves he seeks, though vainly he
    aspire.
Somewhere is knowledge ; did we only toil
At thought, as meaner labourers at the soil,
Then might we our lost strength renew,
And even the hidden wilderness subdue,
Feeding its fallow to its fullest greed
With our primeval germ, as with prolific seed.
Then should we touch the orbs divine
That in far darkness, unconceived of, shine.

VOLUPSA.

It never was so save in metaphor
Wherein your mind is rich and mine is poor :
Not truly touch them, Cœlis?

CŒLIS.

With our soul ;
Which is of earth and heaven the one epitome :
A mirror that reflects the whole ;
And loving eyes in it may all things see.
Ah ! could you feel how there the vista brightens,
And reach with me the calm which ever heightens !

VOLUPSA.

Cœlis, I tremble ; if such thoughts have worth
Like us will they enjoy a second birth

When all that we are let to wish will be
Of us a part, like things we daily see.
Our souls are like the butterfly that lives
On what the kind Creator gives ;
It must not seek the flowery heaven before
Its wings are like an angel's. When we soar
Be it alone our Maker to adore !

SCENE III.—*By the Tree of Knowledge. Moonlight.*

CŒLIS, *alone.*

Stiffened in death the things once fair
Under the piercing breezes shiver ;
The moonbeams strike the frosty air
And through its unseen crystals quiver.

CŒLIS.

' Sibyl of Mystery, Soul of the Sky !
Thou speakest in symbols that voiceless are spread
O'er thy dwelling, the star-haunted azure on high ;
That diffused o'er the earth by no mortal are read.
Deeper than sunshine the beams of thy face
Stir man's mystic spirit, yet hold it aloof ;
The thoughts they engender with thine interlace
    To be borne from our reach through the world's
        wondrous roof.
By day we may wander and muse, but its light
Is so real it chides the vain spirit that strives;

More bold are the feelings that blend in thy night,
Pensive Soul ! and with thee into mystery dive.
Thine is the dream-time, the dream without sleep
That poet may enter : ah ! what doth it yield ?
He watches thy ways in the uppermost deep ;
To emotion, not sense, is thy secret revealed.'

The apple-tree has lost its pride
Though moonlight glitters on its bark,
And rings of phosphorescence slide
Round trunk and branches frore and stark.
Among the ferns its fruits are rotten,
But ruddier than in summer-time
Burst forth the scintillating rings of slime,
Like shooting stars of serpent-fire begotten.
The demon's haunt ! And is he truly here ?
Shall next the fascinating gaze appear ?
The verdurous coil is changing ; now to skin,
Now to round flesh seen quivering within.
The parasite assumes the reptile's strength !
It might a mammoth fold within its length.

CŒLIS, KAUSIS.

'Fear not this everlasting Shape,'
He seems to hear the Serpent say :
' My power, embracing all, can none escape,
But flesh and blood are not my prey.
I am the wisdom wherein ever lies
The naked truth that nature falsifies,
And gilds in hope that with the body dies.

O thou vain searcher! canst thou trace
The lines upon a serpent's skin?
There is the map of thy outgoing race,
That yet afresh seems ever to begin;
There mayst thou learn man's day shall surely end
And with the pregnant Nothing that precedes it blend.'

CŒLIS.

Who art thou, O voiced Serpent, thus encoiled
As when our mother of the fruit partook,
Of her first happiness despoiled,—
As to this day records the holy book!

KAUSIS.

These coils, my prison-house, hold earth's Co-Heir:
Welcome were death; that boon is not for me;
A brighter God looks down on this despair,
This hopeless side of an eternity.
Wouldst thou my lot assume and satiate
Thy thirst for life; the weary days devour,
Which, ere they come, with mocking sameness sate?
Look on these loveless orbs! wouldst thou relieve
Their watch that constant as the waves
In vain the alternating quiet craves
But still goes on without reprieve?
With all coeval are these wakeful eyes:
All they behold and meet no new surprise.
Then envy not their ceaseless watch

That would the uneventful death-wink snatch,
And never more on this stale nature gaze !
They look upon the sun and only glaze
In the dead stare that never dies.
Accursèd vision, which has seen
All that can be, all that has ever been,
Till time itself has ceased to be
And counts as one eternity !
To thee the days are new ; they fall
As unto one who has forgotten all.
Could I forget, and nothing see behind ;—
And cast this skin, and rush into the sun,—
There the untasted, fresh emotion find
As though the world had just begun,
How would I revel in so new a lot,
Fast as the pleasures came, as fast forgot,
Hid from my sense the springs of love and hate,
That at their common source each other desecrate.
But Nature must play on her worthless game,
And only can herself repeat :
Cycle on cycle she is still the same ;
Her ends and her beginnings ever meet.
Then how beneficent the lot of man !
He stretches out his narrow span,
To live a day, a night to rest ;
When tired, to die, and so be doubly blest.
While through uncounted cycles I remain,
Thy race goes out, to yet revive again,
Though not till every grain of sand
Has been the centre of a sun,

And all that forms the sea and land
Has through the universal hour-glass run.
Man's long abeyance, 'tis but as a day;
Death after death appears a moment's sleep,
While time still trundles round with busy sweep,
And glides once more into the olden way.

CŒLIS.

What art thou, Spirit?

KAUSIS.

With the hours I change:
In Nature's toil of ceaseless ebb and flow
I turn the tide, that else would onward range
And immortality on all bestow.

CŒLIS.

Breathless, I doubt thee, who wouldst arrogate
To thy cold will the balancing of fate.
There is a Power beyond thee; to her call
My spirit answers, rescued from thy thrall.

KAUSIS.

She hath her separate realm; what is to be,
Throughout all contest, is foreknown to me:
The antagonist I am in double destiny.

CŒLIS.

O Psyche! 'tis not thus!

KAUSIS.

Even she who keeps
The sun and stars,—eternally she weeps
Her unrequited love, that fails at last,
And in the vortex at my call is cast.
She is the sympathetic Soul
Whose light I feel enwreathe the icy pole.
'Tis only there we meet, or we might breed
Death-worlds, but beauteous, from our common seed,
Of whose charmed being none should taste, and none
With eyes that love and wonder, look upon !
But, change must triumph ; the hard firmament
To thee so high, is to my purpose bent ;
Its seeming beauty burns and wastes ;
And to a long decay its transient glory hastes.
Yon moon that doth thy inmost spirit stir
Is but the death-lamp of a sepulchre ;
Fed by the sun's expiring rays,
To gather up the wrecks of the departed days.

As the soul-charmer ends, the Serpent's train
Has shrunk into the parasite again ;
Its leaf-tipped sprays that loosely hang about,
Like straggling locks, innocuous stand out
In the blue night whose calm the scene invests,
But not the listener's wretchedness arrests.

Scene IV.—*The Castle of Cœlis.*

Cœlis, *alone.*

'Then life, forgetful of its former stages,
Breaks ever forth anew in endless time;
Now resting mid the waste of ages,
Now jubilant in Nature's paths sublime!
Again hath gaped the cavern of thy jaw,
O tongue that launched first knowledge from the tree;
And issues thence the all-enduring law
That life and death in turn must ever be!'
So the Soul-seeker heard the revelation,
That what is loveliest of creation
Springs only from a world's decay;
That all returns again to clay!
'Shall not the heavens,' he asks, 'escape?'
He looks above and sees the Serpent's shape
Where constellations fill those plains of lustre;
But denser seem the timid stars to cluster
And ask of him their secret meaning,
While on the hidden power like infants leaning.
With hope, exalting once, that now debases,
Late through the midnight hours he paces
His armour-haunted corridor,
And there finds rest not any more.
The moonlight through the window glances
On jointed mail and shivered lances,

Kindling the ruby panes, though 'neath the sheen
The Serpent-shield shines ever-green,
Paling the past. There as he lay
Upon his bed his will dissolved away,
And in its place so soft a whisper crept
He took it to his spirit as he slept.
Nigh to his breast the Serpent seemed
To breathe into him all he dreamed,
A fulsome whisper that dissembled,
But pure, unchallenged truth resembled:
His conscious being, weak and fevered,
Like a stray memory from its soul dissevered.
So, prostrate was he, when the Snake once more
His spirit to the tree of knowledge bore.

KAUSIS, CŒLIS.

KAUSIS.

'Where, Worm! is the will that its lot would deny?
Where, Worm! is the will that its lord would defy?
Thou hast crawled from the earth in my daylight to
    die!
Thy people, thy kindred, my worship have spurned;
As I tread upon thee, at my tread who hast turned,
This arm, this one arm of a far-ruling fate,
Shall crush them and thee in the coil of its hate.'

Again to him the words in fragments came,
And ever changed, and ever were the same.

And then he saw the Soul of All
Who held the mighty world in thrall,
With the avenging Snake contend,
Whose venom-scales like sculpture chased,
With Her the circling world embraced,
In strife that time can never end.

When tempests over nature hurry
And sweep down forests in their fury,
Then is he calm ; but storms unnumbered,
As though the universe must cease,
Crowded within him while he slumbered,
And all outside reposed in peace.

Scene V.—*The Hall of Voragine.*

Volupsa, Cœlis.

'I haste to you, Volupsa ; let me hear
Your voice in its dear, human melody !
Give mine ears shelter ; save mine eyes the glare
Of hideous visions whence to you I fly.
To the enchanted haunts I go no more ;
Let me through you my ill-timed life explore.'
So Cœlis speaks ; Volupsa says :
'What ails you ? Strangely sounds your speech ;
Though it be kind, its wilderment effrays
The love I bear you, to its inmost reach.'

CŒLIS.

What ails me, ask not! would you hear it
And suffer in this peril too?
Though I told all I yet must bear it;
'Tis not for one so loved to share it;
My trying lot falls not on you.
What ails me? Not the body's ill :
It is a malison in serpent shape,
That never mortal shall escape,
Entwines itself about my strangled will.

VOLUPSA.

O Cœlis!

CŒLIS.

Call me by the name no more ;—
Call me the Last Laocoon!
The Serpent's eyes on me have shone
As glared they on the priest of yore.

VOLUPSA.

Cœlis! can I not calm you?

CŒLIS.

I am calm!
But soothe me with your dimpling cheek ;
Let your soft eyes in light my soul embalm,
That through them I may see the things I seek.

VOLUPSA.

Yes, I will smile.

CŒLIS.

Such smile avert;
It draws not soul to soul in love's desire :
Your lips seem with a snake begirt!
The flame of love is clear ; I see but smouldering
    fire.

VOLUPSA.

Cœlis, be calm, be strong! Repeat
To me the ills you suffer; often
When nothing else a grief can soften,
Fond souls in unison may meet.

CŒLIS.

Shall I relate how one who drank
At nectar-springs, 'neath the foamed poison sank?
And what a gulph now underlies
The heaven where hope ere it has blossomed dies!
Yet sought I not the awful one,
Whose words, whose aspect froze my blood to
    stone!

VOLUPSA.

Yet rest awhile.

CŒLIS.

Rest comes :
This hurried soul it soothes, this pain benumbs.

VOLUPSA.

How so?

CŒLIS.

You do not hear the music throbbing;
It brings me peace ; the rage abates :
You cannot hear the fitful sobbing
That on the burst of rapture waits.
No soul so modulates its mortal voice !
The fall, the rise, the all-resistless swell
That holds emotion's wondrous argument,
Sways hidden nature with its conquering spell :
Absent is word, is thought, is doubt, is choice,
All heavenward lost in this divine consent !
As in a tranquil sleep we choose
Our dreams from things whereon we love to muse,
I call on her who o'er the forest hovers ;
It is her voice that to my senses cleaving,
I hear from holy depths upheaving
A music she alone to me discovers.

VOLUPSA.

What voice? what can this rapture mean?

CŒLIS.

The voice of Psyche, Nature's only queen !
It is not human ; o'er the wintry rime
It floats into the summer-time ;
It lifts me to the place afar
Where the pure hope-blossoms are.

It is a voice that love-attuned pursues me ;
That, when I question, bursts into a song.
Why doth it not to you belong
Who with your gentle love suffuse me?
Then through the mirror of your mind
Might I the never-ending prospect find.

VOLUPSA.

Cœlis! I am so wretched!

CŒLIS.

You elude
This search for life ; only my miseries
In you, as in a second mirror, rise ;
On them, again, within your soul I brood.

VOLUPSA.

I leave you, Cœlis.

CŒLIS.

Stay !

VOLUPSA.

But not to hear
More than a woman's heart can bear?

SCENE VI.—*The Chamber of Volupsa.*

VOLUPSA, *alone.*

Cœlis, in the true mirror of her eyes
Sees but the nimbus-cloud that on him lies.
There with no steady look can he survey
The love she suffers : her perturbèd mind
Can have no peace, no shelter find,
And never more to him its wealth display.
She in the storm of love is overtaken ;
An ever-trembling aspen, tempest-shaken!
He loves her, but he deems her mortal still,
Or would she take no heed of pain,
But rise, upborne on his aspiring will
That cannot of itself all love attain.
How, calm-eyed, could she with her smiles reveal
To him the prospect of an endless weal?
How could she, when his lips so tremble,
Feign that her heart was light and gay;
Her inmost sympathy dissemble ;
In merry tones shut out his soul's dismay?
The cloud that is upon his face
Falls o'er her eyes: can she his pains control ?
O could one look of joy his dreams displace,
Then might he pierce the vista of her soul !
Yet comes a moment that allays
Her pangs, she sings to God, and singing to Him,
  prays.

'The heavenly choirs to Thee belong,
Thou hearkenest to their holy song
Whose melody is Thine.
Then listen to a maiden's prayer;
The throbbings of her anguish bear,
That beat against Thy shrine.

'Though far he wander from my heart,
Let not his love from me depart;
For Thou art distant too,
And fetchest me when I would pray,
And teachest me what words to say,
With contrite heart and true.

'When all is told beyond the sky,
Then can he not the love deny
That from his bosom springs,
As doth Thy holy bird, the Dove,
When it the message of Thy love
To my lone sorrow brings.'

ACT III.

Scene I.

The Soul of Kausis.

Spring breaks ; it is the Serpent's time for treading
His heaven of dank and narrow alleys,
Where he his needle's eye is threading
To sow his hate among the distant valleys.
There eager warriors, whose soil
The troops of Voragine had made their spoil
In war's disastrous play of sword and fire,
Pause in the passion of debate,
And but the Serpent's oracle await,
That rich in easy, subtle thought
Must now the thirst of vengeance sate
In foes who drink at conscience, staking nought.
'Twill tell them how the strong to shake
And in their triumphs overtake
By wiles the Serpent only can invent,
Of lofty seeming but of base intent.
So shall the conquered their new Spring begin :
While the corn grows gathering the fruits of sin.

The inside of a Serpent-Temple in the burnt Forest.

HAVUS *and others, before the Idol.*

HAVUS.

O Kausis, why hast thou forsaken me?

KAUSIS.

Thou hast proclaimed the Cross.

HAVUS.

Not wilfully,
But with that sign of peace to be avenged—

KAUSIS.

Vengeance is mine.

HAVUS.

To be avenged in thee.

KAUSIS.

What boon demand ye at this sacrifice?

HAVUS.

To be as gods and slay our enemies.

KAUSIS.

Only through Death, robed in the flowing blood
Of thy own son.

HAYUS.

The bleating lamb is here;
Yet, be it as thou wilt.

KAUSIS.

Thy son shall die.

HAYUS.

Thy will encompasses
Our weak affections: touch us, that our blood,
Chilled at death's edge, be in its altered course
Numb to remorse. This hand shall loose the stream
Of that dear life.

KAUSIS.

Bear him unto the Tree,
And spear his side; in his last agony
Prophetic, shall he soothsay in thine ear
The one, the certain way.

HAYUS.

Friends, lead him thither,
But blind him, lest he see his father's face.

KAUSIS.

So shall the avenging father through his son
Behold his wish accomplished.

HAYUS.

Be it done.

KAUSIS.

In him the blood of innocence is spilt
To heighten vengeance on another's guilt,
And while his darkness spreads o'er all the land
His inward sight shall more and more expand
To the near future, and its secret know,
And he shall whisper with his dying breath
Such knowledge as can only be in death.
Three days thy son shall sojourn in the grave,
Then shall he rise and his loved people save :
He goes before thee ; on his path attend
And with thee shall he tarry to the end.

    So, scripture-tongued the Serpent's voice prevailed,
And only one the sacrifice bewailed.

HAYUS.

The oracle is closed, but heard the prayer :
Give the dear victim to a father's care ;
Only to me will he his soul declare.

PEOPLE.

Hail, King of the Ophidians !

    Hayus wept.
His heart in that last pang of anguish dead,
The father of the martyr bowed his head,
And the last tear he ever shed
From his deep-purposed brow with trembling
    fingers swept.

SCENE II.—*The Hall of Voragine.*

VOLUPSA, CŒLIS.

Henceforth is Cœlis calm; his panic o'er,
With gentle words would he restore
The wreath of smiles Volupsa wore,
When, in its soul-beams lit, her happy face
Was charged with every sudden grace.
What, thought he, can that wreath replace !
But she had newer smiles that broke
Around her lips even ere she spoke.

CŒLIS.

Volupsa ! scarce I know your face again !
Joyous or sad, 'tis always more than fair ;
But smiles it hath to-day that entertain
Some favoured guest and all love's welcome bear.
What do I see ? the lights within your eyes
Have flashed not so this many a day ;
Lustres of brilliance they display ;—
Your very soul-depths seem to crystallise.

VOLUPSA.

Joy, Cœlis, is of many hues :
You have not heard the cheering news.

My brother has returned; the war
Is closed, our foes are friendly near and far.

CŒLIS.

Tidings of joy, if strife be at an end!

VOLUPSA.

And now my brother pants to greet his dearest friend.

CŒLIS.

When did he come?

VOLUPSA.

It was as morning broke:
Hundreds of villages awoke
In time to hail his gorgeous cavalcade,
And wreaths of common hedge-flowers many made;
Myrtle boughs and laurels waving,
And on the road the cry of victory raving.
Escorted by his guard up to the gate
His honoured name three times the soldier shouted.
He only said it was their bravery won
The glory and the rebels routed:
He gave the triumph to their arms alone.

CŒLIS.

Where is the army now that he commanded?

VOLUPSA.

It is dispersed : the troops are all disbanded,
No longer needed in the field,
So surely is the quarrel healed.

CŒLIS.

Now be it mine a cheering word to say :
My sister Vivia comes to-day ;—

VOLUPSA.

Another joy !

CŒLIS.

She is already on her way.

VOLUPSA.

The happy time for all sets in ;
And now I hear my brother, Voragine ;
That is his step along the corridor :
You know his light and rapid tread !
It is upon the welcome floor,
The home where he was born and bred.
Farewell, awhile !

CŒLIS, *alone.*

The passion of a child :
Oh ! what true music has a sister's love !
About my heart by her 'twas early wove,
Since of its intertwining blisses spoiled !

Scene III.—*The Hall of Voragine.*

Voragine, Cœlis.

Cœlis.

My kinsman, Voragine! A cheerful sight.
You look so firm within your mail,
Few such a living stronghold would assail.

Voragine.

It is but health braced by sword-exercise,
The tonic of the soul! In honest fight
The secret of a man's endurance lies.

Cœlis.

The schooling of the body to the mind.
Ill-trained for such high cult is he
Who what he is not seeks to be:
Oft in the dusk of thought we find
No path to final victory.

Voragine.

What need we more than fame and wealth
In life's short play, and both are yours.
Though, says report, you take by stealth
What open war to me secures.

CŒLIS.

How, then, by stealth ; though said in jest,
It is most covertly expressed.

VORAGINE.

'Tis told no planet passes on parade
But that you rob it of an omen.
So is heaven-brigandage your trade,
As mine to take the lives of foemen.
As you coax nature to reveal
The mighty purpose of her next decreeing,
More fairly from a damsel's heart I steal
The inmost secret of her being.

CŒLIS.

Say it is so : you ever must pourtray
Your humour in a soldier's way.

VORAGINE.

Your fairy sister, Vivia, where is she?
Still in the convent at her training?
Ah ! would she waft her love to me,
And spare me all this heart-complaining !
Now, Cœlis, draw the shadowy moon
Into some shallow pool, and trace
The magic circles : bid her solve
How many months she must revolve
Ere Vivia shall assume her bridal place !
But say we must be wedded soon.

CŒLIS.

She yet is young: but you have long been plighted;
Bid her then solve the riddle that has riven
So many far asunder when united:
So many into madness driven.

VORAGINE.

It may be so when love is little wise,
And takes the gulph ere it can scale the steep ·
Before us shall no obstacle arise,
But that the dancing of our eyes
May in a moment over-leap.
What charm is there like soldier's prattle ;—
The gallant rush, the flash of battle ;—
No maiden heart can this withstand !
To tales of danger while she listens,
The jewel at her eyelash glistens :
The merry moment is at hand !
Ah ! laugh we must not, save at greeting—
To show our joy at such a meeting !
Who has seen battles won and lost
Is slow of victory to boast,
And for the conquest of a maid,
The more he loves the more is he afraid.

CŒLIS.

Love is the hardest of all creeds,
All are its martyrs, wheresoe'er it leads.

VORAGINE.

Vivia is love; no better creed I choose:
But till she comes we must the hours amuse.
Shall we then fence to while away the time?
My thoughts lie near, yours ever are sublime.
I must invent some game to waste the days,
Or they will never flit: I cannot watch,
With you, mild nature's slow, ecstatic ways,
And at set times her inspirations snatch.
Let us begone and with wild pleasure
Race, while the world goes round in stately leisure.

CŒLIS.

Life will go on,—the eagle's speed
It doth not for its squandering need;
But Vivia comes to-day, along the road
Her barb now bears its lightsome load.

VORAGINE.

Such news would cheer an army! Let us spend
The morrow with you; love alone
Can for the misery of those wars atone:
Be it the assurance of their happy end.

CŒLIS.

And from my brother Pandolph is a letter:
A longer one had pleased me better.
'Cœlis,' he says, 'take choice among the fair,

Or Beatrice may plague you with an heir.
Wedded at last I long to show
My charming princess at the old chateau.
So think of us as on our homeward way ;
Perhaps not many hours shall we delay.
Time after time has this been my intent,
But our old oracle not yet is spent ;
For, I had a presentiment.'

VORAGINE.

The best of news.

CŒLIS.

Presentiments we heed,
Though little argument have they to plead.
Perchance my brother feels afar
The signs that move us not when they are near,
And so may he his safety find in fear :
But this must not our pleasure mar,
When all the rest, perhaps Vivia, now are here.

VORAGINE.

Ere the day passes Vivia must I see ;
And on the morrow,—

CŒLIS.

Then the feast shall be.

Scene IV.

Voragine, Volupsa.

VOLUPSA.

How long the time has dragged ; and yet a year
Is gone !

VORAGINE.
Another comes.

VOLUPSA.

You now will stay,
For slowly fills the gap wherein your absence lay.

VORAGINE.

You are not happy, child.

VOLUPSA.

My loneliness
Still weighs upon me, as on you the stress
And hurry of the war.

VORAGINE.

How well divined :
I spend my nights in battle, though my sword
Hangs idly by my bed. That busy sleep !
While I am couched and feel my head indent

The very pillow, I direct the steps
Of my foregoing self into the fight,
And move with it, recumbent though I be,
Into the thick of battle.

VOLUPSA.

So with me:
Upon my spirit hangs the lonely year !

VORAGINE.

Has it been, then, so sad?

VOLUPSA.

Both sad and smiling:
Hope seasoned by its fruits that ripen not.
But you are here.

VORAGINE.

Even mine is not the love
That Cœlis bears you?

VOLUPSA.

Yes ; a brother's love ;
Deeper than all : not more.

VORAGINE.

You have my heart.

VOLUPSA.

You have but half of mine ;
The rest is torn to shreds.

VORAGINE.

Is he then cold?

VOLUPSA.

Never ; the ways of men are not his ways :
He deems that we should do the same on earth
As if we were in heaven.

VORAGINE.

How could it be?

VOLUPSA.

With him it is so, save that being here,
A mortal, a lone wanderer, he seeks
For the unseen like one who searched the world
For some lost friend.

VORAGINE.

And he encounters nought.

VOLUPSA.

Would it were so ; alas ! by day and night
The shadowy Serpent lies upon his path ;
Its threats almost unseat his faculties,
Till comes the calm, when teems the unwhispering air
With revelations of immortal song.

VORAGINE.

Can it be thus? 'Twere supernatural!

VOLUPSA.

So is it to his sense.

VORAGINE.

The mood will change.
When I take Vivia's hand yours must he claim,
Love spreads with such infection; they who fly
Are the first overtaken by its plague.
A single wedding is the fruitful core
Of countless marriage feasts.

VOLUPSA.

'Twill need no veil
To hide my blushes that can never bloom
Before an altar. All my thoughts to his
Prove adverse; my poor love cannot fulfil
The wealth of his affection, though its flame
Will not go out, but, like a servile lamp,
Burn by his side in solitude.

SCENE V.—*The Castle of Cœlis.*

CŒLIS, *alone.*

CŒLIS.

O dream that comes to pass when infant truth
Quickens within the vision ! So is born
Divinity to this love-founded world !
It have I sought through crystal depths that lie
In woman's heart, but not before have found
Her mirror open, till this very hour
All is revealed, through her, my holy bride !
The darkness left me when my welcomed eyes
Entered Volupsa's with that sister's joy
Beaming upon them ! How a sister's love
Thus at a brother's kindled, sets at nought
All passion ! On a long-lost heaven beyond,
Through the wide-open window of her soul
My eyes have gazed, and taught me to forego
The one too fond desire that dissipates
The ecstasy of being. O beloved !
How should I touch thy lips, how bruise the bloom
That lies upon them, tender as a dew
On the dimmed ruby ! Like the violet
Kissing the stream, so shall thy lips, that blood
Of grapes has never stained, be left to sip
Heaven's nectar ; while henceforward I invoke
Thy sister-love, pure, and unchangeable,
From infant days to age. Belovèd one,
Ideal sister ! be our bridal vows

In bonds held chaste for yet a little while :
What I now feel draws our hereafter near.

CŒLIS, VORAGINE, VIVIA, VOLUPSA.

(VOLUPSA *and* VIVIA.)

VOLUPSA.

My own red Rose !

VIVIA.

My Lily of the Vale!

VOLUPSA.

Your cheeks, how blooming !

VIVIA.

Yours, why are they pale ?

(CŒLIS, VOLUPSA.)

CŒLIS.

See you yon shadow from the mountain steeps
That swiftly o'er the primrose-valley sweeps?

VOLUPSA.

It seemed to rush away between
The hanging rocks, and to be no more seen.

CŒLIS.

So is it with us here ; could we remain,
Or find, at once, the ever-shining plain,
Life would be real ; that which has its close
Begins not: all is but a mocking flight,
Before and after swallowed up in night
Whence like a flitting shadow it arose.

(VORAGINE, VIVIA.)

VORAGINE.

Yes, long the land 'neath war's hard grasp has chafed,
But, like your smiles, is peace to me vouchsafed;—
And now my thoughts on better days are set :
A soldier's utmost need is to forget.

(CŒLIS, VOLUPSA.)

CŒLIS.

So vanishes all love if, soul to soul,
It be not graved on the eternal roll.
There be our plight and heaven emblazon it !

VOLUPSA.

There has my love this many a day been writ.

(VORAGINE, VIVIA.)

VORAGINE.

Yet is life long; though spent with you 'twould run
Swift to the end, as though 'twere just begun.

VIVIA.

That were too fast, if 'twere for me to choose.

VORAGINE.

Then let us not the passing moment lose!

(CŒLIS, VOLUPSA.)

CŒLIS.

Can you then love me for the after-time,
That singly, yet as one, our souls may climb
To times immortal; only there to blend
In that existence which shall never end?
It will surpass this world!

VOLUPSA.

I do so now;
To me this life has long been only vain,
Yet does my lasting love for you remain.

CŒLIS.

Those holy words indite our final vow!

(VORAGINE, VIVIA.)

VORAGINE.

Yes, you are young : the younger be my heart,
That it may cling to yours till death us part.

VIVIA.

Let me die first; it is but once we die.

VORAGINE.

No, you must keep alive my memory !

(CŒLIS, VOLUPSA.)

CŒLIS.

Will you, Volupsa, at your parting breath
Think of our vow, that when we conquer death
We shall arise as one ?

VOLUPSA.

Then, what has brought
A love so deep across your dubious thought?
Am not I constant, when one only prayer
Leaves my sad heart for Heaven ; that you may
    love me there ?

ACT IV.

Scene I.—*The Banquet-room in the Castle of Cœlis.*

Cœlis, Voragine, Volupsa, Vivia.

Within those legend-bearing walls
Whose age the world's great age recals,
Two blushing maids with love elate
By Voragine and Cœlis sate,
All feasting there in high baronial state.
The warrior now has doffed his crest;
No armature is on his breast;
He revels in his well-earned rest.
A feast of love! Some long-gone day
Drawn back into the happy scene
They tell of in such merry way
That much seems left of what has been.
Then startled, all have ceased to speak:
Sounds of sweet music on them break.
A Minstrel at the gate is singing,
The harp rebounds, the wires are ringing
As he, the deep-voiced Troubadour,
Attunes them to the tale of war.

What words he utters well he feels,
And to the warrior his song appeals!

'"Twas at the meeting of the dead
The fallen bade our slaughters cease;
We mourned their blood that we had shed,
We hailed the better day of peace,
And now one boon we ask that Heaven
Hath ever to the wretched given.'

The words were few but many times
O'er varying keys he spread the rhymes.
The warrior was at Vivia's side :
She shed the tears that he must hide,
Sad in the sorrow of the song;
While deep emotions in him throng
At some awakened sense of wrong.
For lands had he to deserts turned,
And herdsmen slain, and many dwellings burned.
Volupsa watches every thought
The Minstrel's words o'er Cœlis brought,
Thinking, in her silent woe,
Her brother's love would from her turn
To Vivia, and that Cœlis yet might spurn
The heart she gave him long ago.

Now the Minstrel sings again,
And in the same soul-searching strain.
All hasten to the gateway fain to hear
What they may lose not being there.

They gather on the parapet
Where valleys dip and mountains rise
Around a poet's paradise ;
Where strangest deeds may happen yet.
O Minstrel ! Canst thou prophesy ?
Peace is to-day and war is of the past !
But curses every blessing underlie,
And all things bend before a winter's blast.

SCENE II.—*The Gate of Cœlis.*

CŒLIS, VORAGINE, VOLUPSA, VIVIA, *and* HAVUS, *as a Troubadour.*

' Begin once more,' the warrior says :
' Not oft such music greets our ears ;
Your song hath left this maid in tears.'
With grateful looks the bard obeys.
The warrior lists as through him rings
The growing burden of the verses
Which the grand Troubadour rehearses,
And to the depths of anguish sings.
The warrior knew his arms had spread
Dismay where hosts but live to mourn the dead :
The wife and child together slain ;
The bride hair-dragged to slaughter, screaming ;
Her prayer unheard, poured out in vain;
Then her young blood in silence streaming.

VORAGINE.

What is your story, Minstrel?

HAYUS.

I, alone,
Am left of the true bards for ever gone,
Of the old Troubadours descended,
Whose days but not whose songs have ended.
They rise up from the buried time,
And story lives in monuments of rhyme.
Men seldom now the minstrel hear;
Ghost-like he passes o'er his father's track
And for a moment flashes back;
Ere long to wholly disappear.

Cœlis loves the Troubadour,
So human were those deep-set eyes,
That had a troubled look divinely pure;
And kindly thus unto his words replies:

'You can our hearts already read;
There seek your welcome; speak your need:
What is it brings you to the door?'

HAYUS.

I will be bold; affairs of state
Have brought me to this noble house;
Our cause I pray all present to espouse!
On this depends my country's fate.
My father was a sacred bard
Whose songs with filial reverence I guard;

With him I roved the distant kingdoms through
Rehearsing newer deeds than yet had flown
O'er homes that to each other were unknown,
And well the legend of this house he knew.
My father taught me reverence for your name :
From that high source my inspiration came !
The Serpent was the guardian of your race ;
And they who braved his anger rued too soon
The woes that once befel Laocoon !
And many shared that victim's throes ;
Not sadder than my own dear country's woes !
So as we spread your fame from place to place,
Of you I ask a boon ; to spare
Our land and take its people to your care.
Myself the leader of a strolling band,
Rare actors every one, and nigh at hand,
I seek the favour first, not hard to grant,
That we may act our play on yonder sward ;
And if our effort please, be our reward
That mercy wakens to our nobler want !

CŒLIS.

Tell us at once your full desire ;
Willing are we to give it heed ;
But first shall we your band of actors hire,
Whatever else may be your pressing need.

HAYUS.

It is that Voragine, your chief, revoke
The impost on our hungry soil :

Conquest has left on us its bitter yoke,
And few remain to sweat and toil.
Humble are we, our people are subdued
And seek to thrive in peace, the only lasting good.

VORAGINE.

The little that you ask shall be conceded,
With all the spoils ; and more, if more be needed.

'Then are you not my country's foe,'
The Minstrel said, and to the chief bowed low.
'Since that all hearts are in our favour stirred,
Let me speak on; speak of your sires whose dust
Here sleeps; of whom are many marvels heard :
And who to legends listens in mistrust?
My fathers to your fathers oft have sung
The weird traditions, true though symbolized,
That to this house for centuries have clung.
Above all wealth are they, above all honours
    prized !
They bear us back into the infant times,
Of virgin lands on earth, and early climes,
Whence men derived their origin obscure ;
Who since into the forest-world have spread
With the traditions of their dead,
Which to these latest days endure.
In a dark hour the whisperer of death
Approached their mother with his glozing breath :
Well they remembered all that mother told
As she wept o'er her Paradise of old.'

The Troubadour's devoted eyes
Rest on the prospect that beneath him lies ;
Then the inviting heaven they slowly gauge
To catch some well-timed thought of its high-
  teaching page.
'Yon Soul of All,' he says, 'had striven
To plan our being free of pain :
She, the Wise-Worker, strove in vain,
Not limitless her power.
Change would arise and change was but Decay;
The night would feed upon the day,
The day the night devour.
Despite her, Nature must the work rehearse,
Else had She swept away this universe
Whose charm alternates only with its curse.
But love within her still prevailed,
Though by the Serpent ceaselessly assailed,
Who, ever pressing on her rear,
Poisons the love-born offerings of the year.
The bloom of her all-fruitful being
She sheds even to the future's farthest date ;
Throughout all time the day foreseeing
When man should lose no more his soul's estate.
Hard was the struggle for our race ;
The fierceness of the tiger was its base,
But reason had a growth self-lifting
Above the common nature of mankind :
Through storms within, through trials drifting,
Still the good and evil sifting,
While loftier rose the wondrous mind.

Oft-times it grew to godlike stature
And won such conquests over nature
As in eternal archives ever shine,
And claim for it an origin divine.
But, as in legend still is rife,
The Serpent with the Soul of All at strife
Was lord of death, ensconced in arm-like shape
That clasped within its many circled coil
The soul that would his will escape
And balk him of his richest spoil.
So speak the legends of old times,
That come to us in their heart-clinging rhymes;
That every ear with sweetness sate,
And, once caught up, none dare adulterate.
All these traditions, nobly sung,
To our great troubadours have clung :
And those which breathe the fame and glory
Of this high house rank first in ancient story.
All who dwell here are of Laocoon's line,
A kingly race, priests of a sun-god's shrine :
But they had foes that never slept ;
And from the sea two jealous serpents crept,
Entwining sire and sons within their grasp,
And still those suffering souls they seem to clasp.
Who gazed, stood in their presence numb,
The tongues of olden bards were stricken dumb ;
But lives the record in that marble rock
Which, thrilled with horror, trembled in the shock,
And, scaling gave to sight the Serpent's skin
And all the direful group that writhed within.

There stood the three in fiery anguish seething,
The knotted Serpents sire and sons enwreathing.'

The maidens hand in hand have met,
With open mouths and brows firm set;
Yet eager and with frighted stare
They listen, though the tale their senses scare.

'The serpents crept through every land,
In one all-tempting purpose clanned :
In forest stretched across from bole to bole
Waiting their prey, the wandering soul,
Were they below the lofty branches slung,
And there in emerald dyes and ruby lustre hung,
Green where the summer boughs were green,
Red where the tangled creepers tinged the autumnal
    scene.
Then could I tell you, ne'er to be forgot,
How the great lords, your sires, were led
By the arch-serpent to this pleasant spot,
Where o'er the gateway still he rears his head,
The mystic symbol of a form
That winds its will about the darting storm.
But these old legends reach so high,
They burn into the page of prophecy,
Where none can loose the fiery letters,
Bound and clasped in iron fetters,
Till, on the dreaded day foredoomed,
They burst in flame and are, with all, consumed.

SCENE III.—*The Chamber of Volupsa.*

VOLUPSA, *alone.*

Though now the Minstrel's tones are hushed,
His sweep of feeling is unstayed :
The torrent from that bosom rushed,
As there he trembled, self-dismayed,
And poured his rage down every ear ;—
Dire threats the spirit's channel tracking
He held all listeners in fear,
As in a fiery ring that burned
Round all, while on themselves they turned,
As with a serpent-sting their bosoms racking.
　　And speedily Volupsa fled ;
Her rest was in her brother's hall ;
There her afflicted heart she read,
Bodings of evil only to recal.
She had the patient gift that dwells
On thought as deeply as on deeds,
And now her heart the meaning tells
Of all that on its quiet feeds.
She looks not forward only, but within
Where ills that are to be so oft begin.
Those records, now, that many deem
The vapid verse of false tradition,
Haunt her as some unusual dream
That glares on her through bars of superstition.

What dare she think? Is he indeed a bard,
Whose songs so on her spirit jarred,
Or but a man of mysteries?
Yet goodness glistened in his eyes!
What semblance sees she, be it dim,
Between the wily Snake and him?
Doth one within the other lurk,
That both such power o'er Cœlis work,
Trailing through bliss his phrenzied aspiration,
While spirits tune some choral hymn,
With stolen notes of seraphim,
And hold his soul in fascination?
She dares not think and but pours forth a prayer,
That God may take her to his care.

'O help of the helpless! who ever art nigh;
The Shepherd on whom in our need we rely,
In whose light are the tears of the wretched made dry;
Look down on this heart, thy poor suppliant behold;
For her sake the loved Lamb to thy bosom enfold!'

SCENE IV.—*Terrace at the Gate of Cœlis.*

VORAGINE, VIVIA.

Vivia as one benumbed was lost in awe,
When Voragine her terror saw :
He said that legends well he loved,
But not a soldier it behoved
To put his trust in what a minstrel sings ;
That faith with him was but in passing things.
Cœlis and the Troubadour
Pass down the slope, the valley to explore,
Where they may commune on the play,
And fix the morrow for the gala-day.
Vivia not long remains in dread
While her fond hand the warrior keeps
In his, as if already wed ;
And there it softly rests as when she sleeps.

VORAGINE

Will not you, sweetest, kindly muse
On my last words? this were not life
Should you my loving heart refuse !

VIVIA.

But I am young to be a wife !

VORAGINE.

Not young the bridal veil to wear!

VIVIA.

I feel that you are brave and kind;
Then something crosses o'er my mind
And makes me pant with sudden fear.

VORAGINE.

Yes, you are young, but were you older
Your timid heart would not be bolder.

VIVIA.

I have so many things to learn;
At school we only write and read:
It will take long my mind to turn
To all a soldier's wife must need.

VORAGINE.

•All he can ask for, you possess;
A gentle heart, a ready thought:
What gifts a soldier's life to bless!
The rest is all by instinct caught.

VIVIA.

Dear Cousin, you will wait at least
Till she knows household duties better?

Suppose that you proclaimed a feast,
Then what confusion would beset her!
When the splendid guests assemble
About you, and your praises sound,
Her cheeks would burn, her feet would tremble
As she were sinking through the ground.

VORAGINE.

Not when a diamond shower has clung
In radiant drops about her neck,
And pearls as thick as hailstones flung
Upon her hair her head shall deck?

VIVIA.

Easy it is for you to bask
In glory, won by you in fight:
It is for me a trying task
To lift my eyelids in your light.

VORAGINE.

Yet when you risk those swaying eyes
And turn their look of love on me,
A voice within my heart replies,
Such bliss on earth can never be!

VIVIA.

Am I so loved? or am I made
The philtre but to work the spell,

The charm soon gone, when I must fade
Into a child, a graceless girl!

VORAGINE.

The gifts and honours that the throne
Confers, may every soldier know :
Your heart is one, the only one,
No monarch can on him bestow.

VIVIA.

Once did I care to see you great
Till love for you has turned my head ;
But we another year must wait ;
You know that I am young to wed !

VORAGINE.

You soon to woman's prime will reach,
Even as the bud its growth extends ;
You then will ask with bolder speech
When this long term of spring-tide ends.

VIVIA.

Tell it to no one for a year !
Our friends would laugh though I should weep :
'Twere long their raillery to bear :
It is a secret you can keep ?

VORAGINE.

You trust it to your faithful slave
Who will your hourly wish obey :
Who would not such a service crave
Awaiting the propitious day !

SCENE V.—*The Paradise of Cœlis.*

CŒLIS, HAYUS.

Along the plain, where seem to grow
Tree-shadows, feeding on the grass below,
Cœlis and Hayus wander, brooding still
O'er serpent-myths and man's mysterious will.
The floods are gone, the brooks are shallow ;
Fields of lilies white and yellow,
That blossomed on the waters' surf,
Have dropped their refuse on the turf.
Spring presses upwards through the grass
That now by sprouting blades is thickened ;
Crisp stems a wealth of flowers amass
'Mid drooping leaves by winter sickened.
' Here,' then said Cœlis, ' act your pleasant play,
And let the morrow be a gala-day.'

HAYUS.

It shall be such a day as few
Can through a life-time see again.

It shall the pastoral times renew
When shepherds ruled as rich a plain.

CŒLIS.

Volupsa loved a pastoral :
May this her early joys recal.
Then Vivia it must needs enrapture :
When her young eyes with pleasure glow
They might a hundred lovers capture.

HAYUS.

The villagers,—

CŒLIS.

Let all attend the show.
A pastoral is the prelude, then,
What follows ?

HAYUS.

Rustic games, when armèd men
Come stealthily as fain to join
Our feast, but would our flocks purloin ;
And while they drive away the cattle
Sound their bugles as for battle.
Our shepherds with their crooks pursue ;
Brief is the struggle, made in vain ;
That day not many do recal ; for few
Escape and many a maid and youth is slain.

CŒLIS.

How ends the play ?

HAYUS.

All for the best,
Though still borne on by passion, deep and strong.
I cannot now describe the rest ;—
All nobly meet the cruel wrong.
Strange seems this answer when you deign to ask
A player how shall end his mimic task ;
But ever has it been our fashion
To yield the climax up to human passion.
Our actors are so gifted that a plot,
Against the impulse of the hour, would fail,
And, as the fury raged, would be forgot :
For genius must o'er all our acts prevail.
How true to nature this ! In many wars
Have served the thoughtful troubadours,
To find in battle's mighty crash
No soldier waits the last command :
Swift inspirations o'er him flash,
And lift his arm and guide his hand.
So is it with our mimic play :
How that may end can no man say.
When once our actors realize their part
The living impulse, only, rules o'er art,
And in their conflicts, soul to Soul,
The first strong act moves onward through the whole.
And well is the spectator pleased :
To guess the plot in vain he tries :
His wonder never is appeased
Till comes the startling end in all its grand surprise.

And now the heart of Hayus torn
By secret pangs beyond itself is borne
Into new anguish, stricken at the thought
That on a friend must vengeance soon be wrought.
Too soon for penitence, too late ;
It cannot bargain 'gainst the rush of fate.
They part, the avenger in the valley stays
Watching, unseen, with ever-deepening gaze
The youth who now ascends the steep and prays.

SCENE VI.—*Hill-side in the Paradise of Cœlis.*

CŒLIS, *alone.*

' On thy darkness, O Sun ! fell the Deity's gaze
And his true image stayed evermore on thy face,
The Soul of thy seasons, the warmth and the l'ght,
To rule this new world that had hung in thy night.
It summoned the forests to feed on its rays :
The flowers it revealed that new-parcelled its blaze
Into yellow thy first, into red thy last hue,
Into heaven's holy curtain the fathomless blue.
O proud Sun ! how thou holdest the virtue divine
That self-shining was left o'er thy empire to shine !
'Twas the first day of thought ; but ere eyes had discerned
'Twas not He in thine orb, but His likeness that burned,—

His glance but the fire-stroke that set thee ablaze,—
We adored thee; to godhead impervious the rays,
That had called up our souls from the passionless night
Soon to learn in their wonder thy might was His might.
We prayed to the forests those beam-germs had sown,
To the Serpent around the huge trunks that had grown
And who guarded the trees wherein wisdom was hidden:
We asked how they spread, how their leaves were secured;
How their flowers and their fruits to the earth were assured,
Though to man's infant soul was such knowledge forbidden.
As His fire when he gazed on thee filled thee with fire
So His likeness sustains our one hope, our desire.
We seek it in Her who still lives in that glance;
Towards Her, its effulgence, our spirits advance;
We seek it in Her to whom rapture belongs:
Who thought after thought the universe throngs.
He is gone; on His way grow the infinite spheres,
And again, save afar, no more he appears,
Ever spreading his glory.'

Now the shallow twilight closes,
And the Soul-seeker, lone, ascends
His mountain slope where he reposes
Watching the sunset till it ends.

Wild colours seeming to have flashed about
And rested flaming, never dying out,
Are piled in heaps discordant and sublime,
The wrecks of day hurled on the molten spires
And burning slow, like mortuary fires;
The yellow floods their reddened rocks o'erflowing,
The orb 'mid wasted embers glowing,
And purple storms behind it blowing
A chaos down the gulph of time.

CŒLIS.

'Spirit of all! My dark winter revive
With thy touch, and restore it to beautiful spring!
To Thee, to thy love, a soul-offering I bring
That where thou inhabitest only can live.'

The last rays melt on the hill-side,
And in them he is glorified.
The white fruit-flowers absorb their hue
As they dissolve to rosy blue,
All in their holy incense dyeing,
While he impurpled on the slope is lying.
The Troubadour alone within the vale
Still watches the Soul-seeker on the height
Changing with nature; pale when she is pale,
Then in her many tints celestial bright.
He sees and lifts his arms up high in air,
His face turned skyward as he muttereth
The secret words of an intense despair
That lies beyond the common pale of death.

ACT V.

Scene I.—*In the Paradise of Cœlis.*

Actors, Spectators.

Sunrise, the constant friend, that ever kept
The appointed time, shone on the Gala-day,
And ere the troop set forth its Serpent Play,
The chilly dews from the arena swept.
So, early, with the heavenly Riser, move
The Minstrel and his Actors on a stage
Where flocks and kine already rove;
Sent there by Cœlis for the lordly sage,
Who with a soul deep-versed in strategy
Can see beyond where eyes can see,
While looking round the chosen plain.
It is his part to improvise,
Where the mock-village is to stand
And streets and temples shall arise;
Where shall rush in the hostile band
Amid the games and with the slain
Cover the earth, while mourners rave
For vengeance or a common grave.

Now the sight-seekers round him gather
With faces smiling at the weather:
A warm spring-morn, as all foretold.
The maids are smart in blue and red
Interlaced with golden thread,
Set off with antique ornaments of gold.
The footmen bring out oaken benches,
A stately butler in their track ;
The handmaids follow, heedless of the clack,
With crimson cushions on their back ;
Jeered at by stable-boys and country wenches.
The peasants still arrive in swarms
That stream in from the distant farms,
With yeomen in their Sunday tunics dressed :
A gala-day their day of rest.

Now harlequins begin to nail
From tree to tree a painted sail,
When houses flutter to and fro
Daubed on the canvas ; then expands
A village o'er the vacant lands,
And soon so real becomes the show
It seems the work of fairy hands.
And where the actors by the score
Are chaffering maids fast knitting at their door,
It seems their native home, so true
Stands out the village in the distant view.

Now Voragine with his elected bride
Vivia, so rosy-cheeked and fair ;
Volupsa leaning at his side,
Descends the castle slope as down a stair,

So serpentine and steep of flight
That thrice they vanish and come back in sight.
Then fifers pierce the lazy ears
But wake a spirit deeper lying,
While drummers shake the heart with fears,
And trumpeters their skill are plying.
At every step full-welcome greets
The chief and maidens, kindly proud,
And serious grows the merry crowd
That bows them to their cushioned seats.

All is prepared, a nation seems to rise
Where woods and pastures only yesterday
Between the sunrise and the sunset lay:
A lone Soul-seeker's Paradise!
The Serpent's haunt, and yet a place of musing
Where brook and ferns had learned to speak;
But not all their silence losing;
Their tongues but known to those who secrets seek.

In chatty groups of three or four
That seem of chance, the actors wait
A signal from the Troubadour,
But, in dumb show, look busied in debate.
Two huntsmen, then, their shoulders laden,
A deer between them forward bear,
And rudely hustle swain and maiden
Who laugh to see the promised fare.
They carry to the front the noble beast,
Now pointing to its antlers, now its haunches,

And short of breath speak of the coming feast,
While each beholder into rapture launches.
There the antlered beauty lies,
As 'twere for some high sacrifice,
Its weeping nostrils like a breath
That sighed out pity for its death.
The tender Vivia feels regret,
Though with her eyes upon the creature set
She longs to have her absent brother near,
Himself to see that lordly forest deer :
' O that his bride and he may yet appear ! '

  The Troubadour now gives the sign
His finger lifting with a scowl malign.
The music answers, and the idlers flow
Into their ranks, then in a double row
With easy paces caper to and fro.
Some pass the bottle while they dance,
The outpoured laughter to enhance ;
Elsewhere village games succeed :
Some hurl the quoit, some run to fetch
The bounding ball they cannot catch ;
Some race in pairs the noble steed.

  But why this sudden change o'er Voragine
Who only scans the painted scene?
His prowess pales, he meets his hour,
Divested of his earthly power !
That scene is but the valley that he smote,
Come to accuse him from its wilds remote,

Yes, he had seen it all before,
And now he knows the Troubadour!
Before his eyes what treachery is bared!
All flashes on him in a deadly throe,
Himself and all his kindred snared,
And at the mercy of a wily foe.
How had he let escape the day
When the proud Minstrel at his mercy lay!
But love is blinding and too fast
The hour of safety from him passed!
They smile at passion who would meditate
How to avert the sluggish tide of fate!

Scene II.—*On the Mount in the Paradise of Cœlis.*

Cœlis; Actors, Spectators, *below.*

To his hill-slope again at break of day
Was Cœlis summoned to fulfil
Within his own some stronger will
That like the weight of love upon him lay.
He dared not mingle in a feast
That was to mock man's pitying thought
For sorrows that had ceased,
Though on the stage once more to memory brought.
Nature, so radiant, gives not back the groan
And lends no sanction to its stern rehearsal;
Though sympathising millions hear the moan,
What once has been has no reversal.

The swelling morn, the living breath,
That all within the clear expanse inhale,
Down from the tumbling mountains to the vale,
These call not back the bitterness of death.

CŒLIS.

' O Psyche, the saviour, in whom we inherit
The gifts of an all-loving, plenteous Spirit,
Who onward for ever thy dream dost pursue ;
Our hope, as we follow, in whom we renew ;
In thy passion immersed all things glow around me ;
On pinions uplifted in bliss thou hast bound me ;
Steeped in thy light, in thy holy emotion,
I drain thy last philtre, the life-giving potion.'

So rapt, he glances o'er the fields :
The dense spectators, the fast-swelling train
Have there no meaning, though his eyes
They vex, and are to him as reveries
That buzz outside the archway of the brain.
There, little earnest, maid and swain
The lover's antics rudely feign,
And care not who rejects or yields.
There they act their courtship dances ;
Near and nearer each advances ;
Swift the music, swift the pace :
So in pairs the lovers drift,
Till all the youths at length uplift
Their arms and ask a maid's embrace.

It was but a re-acted scene ;
But how it smites on Voragine,
When winds the bugle's call defiant
From the lung-clangour of a giant,
And echoes through far-reaching alleys :
The Serpent's track into the hostile valleys !
Those slaughter-sounds,—how like his own
Even to the last high-bounding thrill,
That seemed to summon to his former will
His troops, that dire defeat had never known !
But where was now the army he had led !
Not near to serve him in his narrow strait:
His enemies are now within the gate,
And he their country's blood has shed.

As thus he muses, troops o'er-stride
These scenes of peace, these pastures wide ;
They issue from the wooded lands
To where the flowery vale expands,
And through the dancers spread confusion,
Who act so well their clamourous fear
It needs must be that death is near ;
The mutual fury crushing all illusion.
Are these the troops of Voragine
Clad as were his, and his Cross-banner flying ?
'Tis but in mockery of a former scene !
The women to the soldiers cling,
And for defence their arms about them fling,
But soon in that embrace are dying.

Torch-bearers set the painted scene a blaze,
The pine-trees crackle in the conflagration:
The awed spectators rise and in amaze
Shout out : 'Tis an invading nation !
The Warrior, his sister and his bride
Sit pale; they must the end abide.

The troops drive off the frighted cattle,
As lawful spoil of victors after battle.
The shepherds gather up their dead
And kiss them with hot lips, revenge imbibing,
Then the fresh turf upon the bodies spread.
No home is left, but earth that welters
In the warm blood, the pile accepts and shelters.
This done around the slaughtered crowd the living
And on their spades a fervid oath inscribing,
They brandish them with gestures unforgiving.
And where is Cœlis in that hour? The clang
Of myriad heart-throbs fills him with a pang
Of suffering for all; but panic-held
He waits as by a higher power compelled.
He can interpret all he now beholds ;
He sees one fate his family enfolds ;
Sees that before that bugle blew,
Or Voragine gave challenge throat to throat,
Those slaughter-sounds the welkin smote,
And that the fields of doom that battle knew,
Fought by the present foes in shadowy fight ;
Rehearsed throughout all time ere they beheld the
    light.

SCENE III.—*A Tent in the Paradise of Cœlis.*

Actors, Spectators.

And yet 'twas this the Troubadour foresaid:
In rustic games and strife the hours had sped.
The second scene begins; in council spent,
With purpose hidden, deep, uncertain,
Even when the players lift the curtain.
There have they pitched a lofty tent
That rises like an alpine height
And hides the battle-field from sight,
By flames made doubly desolate.
While glows the canvas snowy white,
O'er it the Serpent-banner soars
In honour of so great a holiday,
And those of safety reassures
Who deemed the battle scarce a play.
And there the peasant-senators debate.
Hayus within the open tent is seen
Now as a mitred priest of stately mien,
In purple vestment; and he bears
In his right hand a cross of gold,
And at his side a poignard wears
Concealed within his garment's fold.

Outside the tent, meantime, the huntsmen stood
Grasping the knives still dyed in harmless blood.

Fierce, motionless, without a breath,
They kept their eyes intent on Voragine
And his afflicted maiden kin;
With looks that threatened death for death.
Then, cried the Priest with voice that smote
The towers and echoing walls remote,—
' Here the dumb speak, again the murdered feel,
While sufferers to sufferers appeal !'
Then he looked round on many faces
Whereon erewhile was not a care ;
That now are masked in madness and despair.

HAYUS.

Who shall our peace and love restore !
The sire is buried in his field
That shall no harvest to his children yield,
That he shall sow and reap no more.
Let it lie waste, and be a grave
Ye hearts that sorrow and for vengeance crave !

    Afresh the huntsmen grasp their knives
And lift them flashing ! The keen blades
Are aimed no more at harmless lives.
' Ye antlered Stags ! We only chafe
To reach his heart who slew our wives !
Graze on, well-watered be your glades !
Peace be with you ; ah ! you are safe.'
    The Priest lifts up his head once more,
As of a drowning man remote from shore,

And cries, 'Youths, stand you there with brows
   indented?
Can you ever love again
Who saw your first betrothed ones slain;
Is the dark outrage unresented?'
Nigh him a mournful woman stoops :
And as he points the more she droops.
He sees her fidget at her breast;
' There,' cries he, ' did her slaughtered baby rest !'
She starts, she feels it to her cleave,
And its last breath against her bosom heave.

' O my lost people !' cries the Troubadour,
' Revenge is not all balm; let us implore
His solace whom we all adore.
Almighty One,
Lift our hearts gently to thy throne !'

These words the Troubadour strains forth,
All kneel, all eyes on Heaven are bent;
All anger is subdued, all wrath;
Upraised and calm is every face,
And vanishes the boundless space
Between them and the firmament.

HAYUS.

'Supremest Lord,
High on thy olive-branch hang up the sword,
And these dead hearts inspire :
To know thy will is now their one desire !

As suns in-breathed thy will when first they burned,
As stars in-breathed thy will when first they turned
And rushed into the paths Thou didst vacate,
To these dead hearts thy will bequeath
Who now in outer anguish seethe,
But thy commandments venerate.'

  Then knelt in prayer the Troubadour,
But spoke no word, his hands together wringing,
His arms, in his despair, up-flinging
That seemed to lift the graves, and call
On the Most High to witness all !
His eyes in this last pang he raises,
Then flings his body in the dust.
The multitude intensely gazes ;
On them like a blighting gust
His anguish falls : the curtains are descending ;
O'er the closed tent the Serpent-banner strides !
The second scene of this dread Play is ending ;
And no applause the tragedy derides.

SCENE IV.—*The Tent in the Paradise of Cœlis; and, moving round the heights, a car bearing Pandolph and Beatrice.*

Actors, Spectators, Troops.

In sudden haste starts back each flapping sail.
'Where are we?' asks the Minstrel, dazed and pale :
'No longer in His Presence who unrolled
The Will Supreme !'
He shivers in the cold,
Slow to proceed and slow the fiat to unfold.
'No longer in the burning clime above
Where we beheld the God of Love,
As he revealed his mighty will !'
And thus the Minstrel lingers still
Like one death-stricken by an earthly chill,
Although the sun o'er his encampment flame.
And closer draws his robes around,
Trembling in ecstasy profound.
'Beloved, who for your parents mourn,
Friends life-severed, wives from husbands torn,
You have a Father ! His kind grace
You found ; I see it shine in every face ;
All base revenge has passed and left no trace.
Were you all punished for your crimes
Committed in the peaceful times,
And was the visitation sent
For your offences, bidding you repent ?

Or has the wondrous verdict freed
Your lives and no accuser come
To brand you, or to justify the deed
That to those ashes gave your home?'

There still is silence, but resolve is there,
That doth some awful purpose bear.
The Warrior, calm, is yet aghast,
And sits two trembling maids between,
His present ever nearer to his past.

HAYUS.

I know your will; it is His Will : I saw
Unrolled the sentence of His law.
'Tis not revenge, the despicable crime !
For Heaven is high, her verdicts are sublime.
She bids us with our dead to bury hate,
Not on revenge our sorrow satiate !
Not vengeance?

A stern Chorus thunders, ' No !'

The huntsmen then in voices fierce and fell
Cry out, ' This woman shall our verdict tell ;
She smarts beneath the murderer's blow.'
Held up, the woman staggers, sliding
Before the priest as o'er a Serpent's path.
She is the vessel of a stagnant wrath
Which is the flood-time of its grief abiding.

She, once more childless, hides her face
As if so deep a sorrow were disgrace.
She like a dying Pythoness appears :
The pitying audience moans for her its fears.
None hear her voice, she whispers low ;
She shivers in the winter of her woe.
The Priest supports her to the seats,
And to the eager crowd repeats
The few short words the woman said.

'Not in revenge Heaven lifts the rod!'
Thrice from his mouth and ever louder,
His voice more stern his bearing prouder,
Thrice the verdict he delivers,
And every heart there present quivers
As when a text from Holy Writ
A demon's soul in man has lit,
While still is flaming in his eyes
The wrath to come ! How shall it end?
Again his words as bolts descend :
'Not to avenge ! but, to chastise !'
Thus as he cruelly lets fall
The Word of God, it crushes all.
They seem to see in their dismay
An angry God among them at the play,
Who brings with Him his judgment-day.

HAYUS.

Not to avenge, but to chastise !
They who an infant's strength despise,

And on a woman's body trample,
Our God elects for high example.

The Chorus shrilly shouts: 'For ever!'

HAYUS.

Could they our peace of mind restore us
We might forgive : this can they never :
It is an hour of retribution
And for their sin is no ablution.

CHORUS.

For ever blood must wash out blood!

    The Priest less stern, in silence stood,
His people mute ; again his eyes
Fall on them ; every voice replies
In shriller chorus : ' Blood for blood ! '

HAYUS.

Then shall there be three signs from Heaven :
Behold the first !

    The Cross he raises.
As soon as they perceive the signal given
By bugle blast all ears are riven,
That through the distant gorges winds
And hill and vale in echoing tumult binds.
When near the summons ceases to be heard,

Afar, unto the utmost mazes
The chill recesses of the gorge are stirred.
The Warrior dreads, no eye can see
What fearful vengeance is in store:
Yet is it war's fair strategy,
Though he shall shout of victory no more.
Could he the dear loved woman save!
But how? Fierce eyes their every movement follow.
O anguish, must a common grave
The innocent and guilty swallow?
He bids the maidens go; they cannot rise,
Their quivering limbs have not the power,
Held in the terror of that hour;
And death seems glazing in their eyes.

Back from the gorge a trumpet-note
Is thrice repeated, then with sound
Of heavy tramp, confused and loud,
As when deep thunders crush the ground,
The dust advancing cloud on cloud,
All ears as by their destiny are smote.
A troop of horsemen clad for fight
With sabres drawn bursts into sight,
And vultures startled at the bugle-shock,
Flap their disordered wings, and from their rock
Scale with stretched necks the skyey hollow,
And o'er the ill-fated fields the troopers follow.
Between the arena and the hills
That savage band the narrow passage fills;
A panic spreads, by many ways

To make escape the crowd essays,
But all who fly the flashing steel dismays.
Now are there screams and woman's wails,
Terror in every face prevails.
No blow is struck, no threat is spoken;
Each horseman falls into his place,
And thus in line those troops the people face,
Encircling all in ranks unbroken.
Their banner-bearers on white chargers seated
Display the fluttering Serpent to the crowd,
Its blood-red coils, its movements proud,
Now in the troubled ether shaking,
Now over all in frightful billows breaking.

Hopeless, then whispers Voragine
To Vivia : ' Is there aught that you have seen ? '
She answers, ' Pandolph and his Beatrice.'

VORAGINE.

They move along the heights ; they pause ; and now
Dismayed they look upon us from the mountain-brow.
They move again, towards Cœlis winds their car,
As they gaze on us still.

VIVIA.

Let it suffice
That they are safe.

VORAGINE.

They yet may bring us aid ;
If not, their coming has been well delayed.
They vanish now.

VIVIA.

They reappear ; they are
With Cœlis on his mount ; and now their car
Wheels swiftly forward from the danger gone,
And Cœlis, watching us, is there alone.

SCENE V.—*The Paradise of Cœlis.*

Actors, Spectators, Troops, and the Serpent KAUSIS.

The stage into a nation grows ;
The actors swell into avenging foes.
With sadder look the Troubadour
Advances towards the people, hushed,
While he uplifts the Cross once more ;
So drops away their fitful roar
Like falling waves upon the boulders crushed.
Till it befal to learn their fates
The panting crowd his voice awaits :
Some deem that out of such a multitude
They may themselves the crush elude,

While some are smarting and have swooned
Ere they have dropped beneath a sabre's wound.

HAYUS.

'Hear, Voragine! When thou didst lead
Thy arms against us, what was our offence?
Then be the ending of thy deed
A terror for all coming time;
And be the sentence passed upon thy crime
Worse than the pangs of life-long penitence.
I curse thee through the Power above
Whose dearest work thou didst efface;
I curse thee through his utmost love
Who suffered death to spare the human race!
I curse thy kindred and thy bride,
And all who shared in thee a hero's pride!
Our fate we feel; be thine as hard a fate
And like our homes these homes be desolate!
The dogs of war to thee return,
Let loose upon us in that cruel fray;
Again with thirst of blood they burn
On this their second festal day.
So endeth this long-memorable Play!'

He lifts the Cross a third time, at whose flash
He turns his face, then out of sight retires,
But in departing hears the armour's crash.
The watchful troops had caught the sign
And in their bosoms wrath divine
The rage of vengeance fires.

The horsemen in their fury leap
At helpless crowds and o'er their bodies sweep,
Sabreing alike the old and young.
The people to and fro are driven,
Shrieking for pity never given
By those who trample down the astonished throng.
Some towards the open gates are rushing
To but encounter sights more dire :
The Serpent Kausis guards the gates,
And there his maddened prey awaits,
Rolling o'er them his eyes of fire ;
Their bodies in an instant crushing.

When eyes no longer upward gaze,
Fresh dimmed by death, like fiery snakes outburst
Red flames upon the height accursed,
Swift coils of fire the castle racking,
Like bones its oaken rafters cracking,
Till every house was fuel in the blaze,
That like a sea to the far valley spread
Where Hayus lay, self-smitten, with the dead.

SCENE VI.—*The Hill-side in the Paradise of Cœlis.*

CŒLIS, PSYCHE.

'Neath the mid-torment of soul-rending wails
Cœlis looks down upon the mortal fray :
Then doth he know the Serpent Play
O'er all things great on earth prevails.
He sees, he shudders, thought is as a fire
Struggling to burn in ice, that numbs all pain,
And only leaves a phantom of desire
To call on Psyche now his soul is slain.
He drops as one by death infected
Whose stabs he saw on his loved kindred fall,
And is content to die with all
If to the common lot by fate elected.
Like a cleft elm that screams in falling,
For help on outraged nature calling,
He 'neath the crushing vengeance bends,
And, with a bitter cry, his struggle ends.
So stunned, the Serpent seems to wind
About him and his body bind ;
Closing upon his limbs that break
Like saplings which the winter winds o'ertake,
But know no torture while they crack
In the all-sundering rack.

But he was not to die alone,
For he had found the holy being ;
Through his clear soul the Soul of All foreseeing.

Prostrate, even Her he cannot seek,
Yet 'tis her voice, leading a melody
That covers, as with flowers, the blessed who die.
He feels again; he hears her speak:
The Spirit of death-conquering Spring,
In bridal beauty She is nigh;
And from his vision all past things have gone.
'Tis hope no more; with loving eyes
Doth She the one elixir bring;
He tastes it, and he lives the while he dies.
O Death! is this thy sting?

Where beams in circling courses trace
   The climate of the skies,
And unto Psyche's holy place
   The happy souls arise,
Do loving voices still repeat
Their music round her blessed seat.

The spirits who in watchings long
   This future did behold,
She calls up from the mortal throng
   And leads them to her fold.
On their soul's lyre her fingers play
The bliss of everlasting day.

   And now the mid-air choirs outpour
The anthem of an Evermore:

'Only the good awake
And gather to the chambers of the Blest!
　　Arise ye holy and partake
The soul's high gift; once known for aye possessed!
　　Only the pure arise!
Only the wicked stay below at rest,
　　Self-exiled from the skies,
Forgetful as the ground-mist that beneath
Feedeth the worms' cold breath.
　　High souls death's rusty fetters break,
　　To the new life awake,
And gather to the chambers of the Blest!'

What senses now from earthly senses surge!
His soul creates; from him all things emerge.
He thinks of Psyche; her encircling streams
Of pointing light strike to the shaded skies;
He thinks of his Volupsa; the same beams
Pass through her as he gazes in her eyes
Which steeped in human love before him shine,
Their sympathy the speech of intercourse divine.
The heavens are measureless, the dead are free;
With their brief day on earth their sorrows cease.
O Grave, this is thy victory;
O Soul, this is thy peace!

[October, 1882

CHATTO & WINDUS'S
LIST OF BOOKS.
₊ For NOVELS, see pp. 19-25.

Beautifully bound in a novel style, small 4to, 16s.
THE LADY OF THE LAKE. By Sir WALTER SCOTT. With numerous fine Illustrations.
"*The Lady of the Lake* " *has been chosen as a subject for illustration, not only for its picturesque features, which invite in an unusual degree the sympathetic treatment of the artist, but also for the romantic personal interest which the story inspires, and which gives it a close hold on the affections of all readers. So thorough is the verisimilitude of the poem, and so accurate are its descriptions of scenery, that the events which it describes are accepted as absolute history in the region where the scene is laid; and no true Highlander looks with tolerance on anyone who ventures to doubt their actual occurrence. It has happened, therefore, that the romantic poem in which the genius of Scott has united and harmonised the legends of Loch Katrine and the Trosachs has become the best Handbook to the Scottish Lake-region. It is believed that the present Illustrated Edition will be a welcome souvenir to thousands of travellers who have visited that beautiful region.*

In order to secure accuracy as well as freshness of treatment, the Publishers commissioned Mr. A. V. S. ANTHONY, *under whose supervision this Edition has been executed, to visit the Scottish Highlands and make sketches on the spot. Nearly every scene of the poem was personally visited and sketched by him, and these Sketches have afforded the basis of the landscapes offered in this book. These landscapes, for obvious reasons, depict the Scenery as it is at the present time; while the Costumes, Weapons, and other accessories of the figure-pieces are of the period of the action of the poem, being carefully studied from contemporary pictures and descriptions, or from later authoritative works.*

Crown 8vo, Coloured Frontispiece and Illustrations, cloth gilt, 7s. 6d.
Advertising, A History of,
From the Earliest Times. Illustrated by Anecdotes, Curious Specimens, and Notices of Successful Advertisers. By HENRY SAMPSON.

Allen (Grant), Works by:
The Evolutionist at Large. By GRANT ALLEN. Crown 8vo, cloth extra, 6s.
Vignettes from Nature. By GRANT ALLEN. Crown 8vo, cloth extra, 6s.
"*One of the best specimens of popular scientific exposition that we have ever had the good fortune to fall in with.*"—LEEDS MERCURY.

Crown 8vo, cloth extra, with 639 Illustrations, 7s. 6d.
Architectural Styles, A Handbook of.
From the German of A. ROSENGARTEN, by W. COLLETT-SANDARS.

Artemus Ward:
Artemus Ward's Works: The Works of CHARLES FARRER BROWNE, better known as ARTEMUS WARD. Crown 8vo, with Portrait and Facsimile, cloth extra, 7s. 6d.
Artemus Ward's Lecture on the Mormons. With 32 Illustrations. Edited, with Preface, by EDWARD P. HINGSTON. 6d.

Ashton (John), Works by:
A History of the Chap-Books of the Eighteenth Century. By JOHN ASHTON. With nearly 400 Illustrations, engraved in facsimile of the originals. Crown 8vo, cloth extra, 7s. 6d.
Social Life in the Reign of Queen Anne. Taken from Original Sources. By JOHN ASHTON. With nearly One Hundred Illustrations. Two Vols., demy 8vo, cloth extra, 28s. [In preparation.

Crown 8vo, cloth extra, 7s. 6d.

Bankers, A Handbook of London;
Together with Lists of Bankers from 1677. By F. G. HILTON PRICE.

Bardsley (Rev. C. W.), Works by:
English Surnames: Their Sources and Significations. By the Rev. C. W. BARDSLEY, M.A. Crown 8vo, cloth extra, 7s. 6d.
Curiosities of Puritan Nomenclature. By the Rev. C. W. BARDSLEY, M.A. Crown 8vo, cloth extra, 7s. 6d.

Crown 8vo, cloth extra, Illustrated, 7s. 6d.

Bartholomew Fair, Memoirs of.
By HENRY MORLEY. New Edition, with One Hundred Illustrations.

Imperial 4to, cloth extra, gilt and gilt edges, 21s. per volume.

Beautiful Pictures by British Artists:
A Gathering of Favourites from our Picture Galleries. In Two Series. All engraved on Steel in the highest style of Art. Edited, with Notices of the Artists, by SYDNEY ARMYTAGE, M.A.

Small 4to, green and gold, 6s. 6d.; gilt edges, 7s. 6d.

Bechstein's As Pretty as Seven,
And other German Stories. Collected by LUDWIG BECHSTEIN. With Additional Tales by the Brothers GRIMM, and 100 Illustrations by RICHTER.

One Shilling Monthly, Illustrated.

Belgravia for 1882.
A New Serial Story, entitled "**All Sorts and Conditions of Men**," by WALTER BESANT, was begun in the JANUARY Number, which Number contained also the First Chapters of "**The Admiral's Ward**," by Mrs. ALEXANDER; and the First of a Series of Papers "**About Yorkshire**," by Mrs. MACQUOID, Illustrated by THOMAS R. MACQUOID.—In the AUGUST Number was begun a New Story by WILKIE COLLINS, entitled "**Heart and Science.**"—In JANUARY, 1883, will be begun a New Serial Novel by JUSTIN MCCARTHY, entitled "**Maid of Athens**," with Illustrations by FRED. BARNARD.

Belgravia Annual.
With Stories by WALTER BESANT, JULIAN HAWTHORNE, F. W. ROBINSON, DUTTON COOK, JUSTIN H. McCARTHY, J. ARBUTHNOT WILSON, HENRY W. LUCY, JAMES PAYN, and others. Demy 8vo. with Illustrations, 1s. [In November.

CHATTO & WINDUS, PICCADILLY. 3

Demy 8vo, Illustrated, uniform in size for binding.
Blackburn's (Henry) Art Handbooks:
Academy Notes. 1875. With 40 Illustrations. 1s.
Academy Notes, 1876. With 107 Illustrations. 1s.
Academy Notes, 1877. With 143 Illustrations. 1s.
Academy Notes, 1878. With 150 Illustrations. 1s.
Academy Notes, 1879. With 146 Illustrations. 1s.
Academy Notes, 1880. With 126 Illustrations. 1s.
Academy Notes, 1881. With 128 Illustrations. 1s.
Academy Notes, 1882. With 130 Illustrations. 1s.
Grosvenor Notes, 1878. With 68 Illustrations. 1s.
Grosvenor Notes, 1879. With 60 Illustrations. 1s.
Grosvenor Notes, 1880. With 56 Illustrations. 1s.
Grosvenor Notes, 1881. With 74 Illustrations. 1s.
Grosvenor Notes, 1882. With 74 Illustrations. 1s.
Pictures at the Paris Exhibition, 1878. 80 Illustrations. 1s.
Pictures at South Kensington. With 70 Illustrations. 1s.
The English Pictures at the National Gallery. 114 Illusts. 1s.
The Old Masters at the National Gallery. 128 Illusts. 1s. 6d.
Academy Notes, 1875-79. Complete in One Volume, with nearly 600 Illustrations in Facsimile. Demy 8vo, cloth limp, 6s.
Grosvenor Notes, 1877-1882. A Complete Catalogue of Exhibitions at the Grosvenor Gallery since the Commencement. With upwards of 300 Illustrations. Demy 8vo, cloth limp, 6s.
A Complete Illustrated Catalogue to the National Gallery. With Notes by H. BLACKBURN, and 242 Illusts. Demy 8vo, cloth limp, 3s.

UNIFORM WITH "ACADEMY NOTES."
Royal Scottish Academy Notes, 1878. 117 Illustrations. 1s.
Royal Scottish Academy Notes, 1879. 125 Illustrations. 1s.
Royal Scottish Academy Notes, 1880. 114 Illustrations. 1s.
Royal Scottish Academy Notes, 1881. 104 Illustrations. 1s.
Royal Scottish Academy Notes, 1882. 114 Illustrations. 1s.
Glasgow Institute of Fine Arts Notes, 1878. 95 Illusts. 1s.
Glasgow Institute of Fine Arts Notes, 1879. 100 Illusts. 1s.
Glasgow Institute of Fine Arts Notes, 1880. 120 Illusts. 1s.
Glasgow Institute of Fine Arts Notes, 1881. 108 Illusts. 1s.
Glasgow Institute of Fine Arts Notes, 1882. 102 Illusts. 1s.
Walker Art Gallery Notes, Liverpool, 1878. 112 Illusts. 1s.
Walker Art Gallery Notes, Liverpool, 1879. 100 Illusts. 1s.
Walker Art Gallery Notes, Liverpool, 1880. 100 Illusts. 1s.
Royal Manchester Institution Notes, 1878. 88 Illustrations. 1s.
Society of Artists Notes, Birmingham, 1878. 95 Illusts. 1s.
Children of the Great City. By F. W. LAWSON. 1s.

Folio, half-bound boards, India Proofs, 21s.
Blake (William):
Etchings from his Works. By W. B. SCOTT. With descriptive Text.

BOOKS PUBLISHED BY

In Illuminated Cover, crown 4to, 6s.
Birthday Flowers: Their Language and Legends.
By W. J. GORDON. Illust. in Colours by VIOLA BOUGHTON. [*Shortly.*

This sumptuous and elegant Birthday Book is the first in which our floral treasures have been laid under really effective contribution. It has been produced at immense cost, and in it we have one of the most accurate and beautiful Masterpieces of Chromo-lithography yet issued from the press. Within its sixty-four fully-coloured pages, each lithographed in fourteen printings, we have a noble Series of lovely Bouquets, depicting in all their wealth of grace and beauty the most famous of our field and garden jewels; as a different flower is taken for every day in the year, there are no fewer than three hundred and sixty-six separate selections. The legends and the sentiments ascribed to each of the chosen blossoms have formed the theme of some fifteen hundred lines of Original Verse, and there is thus given one of the fullest "Languages of Flowers" in existence, and the only one which is free from duplicates. An unusual amount of thought and labour has been expended on the work, and the publishers congratulate themselves that in a literary and artistic sense the result has been fully commensurate thereto. Such a collection of flowers, so complete and compact, has never before been offered. As a Book of Birthdays and Family Records it is unsurpassed. The addition of the scientific names to the minutely accurate delineations of plants renders its pages invaluable to the botanist and every lover of leaf and bloom. The legends which form the burden of its verse will delight the scholar and archæologist and all students of song and folk-lore; while the copious floral meanings, completer than in any other "language of flowers" yet available, will render it the constant companion and most treasured gift of a much more numerous section of the community—the whole world of Sweethearts of the English-speaking nations.

Crown 8vo, cloth extra, gilt, with Illustrations, 7s. 6d.
Boccaccio's Decameron;
or, Ten Days' Entertainment. Translated into English, with an Introduction by THOMAS WRIGHT, Esq., M.A., F.S.A. With Portrait, and STOTHARD's beautiful Copperplates.

Bowers' (G.) Hunting Sketches:
Canters in Crampshire. By G. BOWERS. I. Gallops from Gorseborough. II. Scrambles with Scratch Packs. III. Studies with Stag Hounds. Oblong 4to, half-bound boards, 21s.

Leaves from a Hunting Journal. By G. BOWERS. Coloured in facsimile of the originals. Oblong 4to, half-bound, 21s.

Crown 8vo, cloth extra, gilt, with numerous Illustrations, 7s. 6d.
Brand's Observations on Popular Antiquities,
chiefly Illustrating the Origin of our Vulgar Customs, Ceremonies, and Superstitions. With the Additions of Sir HENRY ELLIS.

Brewster (Sir David), Works by:
More Worlds than One: The Creed of the Philosopher and the Hope of the Christian. By Sir DAVID BREWSTER. With Plates. Post 8vo, cloth extra, 4s. 6d.

The Martyrs of Science: Lives of GALILEO, TYCHO BRAHE, and KEPLER. By Sir DAVID BREWSTER. With Portraits. Post 8vo, cloth extra, 4s. 6d.

THE STOTHARD BUNYAN.—Crown 8vo, cloth extra, gilt, 7s. 6d.
Bunyan's Pilgrim's Progress.
Edited by Rev. T. SCOTT. With 17 beautiful Steel Plates by STOTHARD, engraved by GOODALL; and numerous Woodcuts.

Bret Harte, Works by:

Bret Harte's Collected Works. Arranged and Revised by the Author. Complete in Five Vols., crown 8vo, cloth extra, 6s. each.
  Vol. I. COMPLETE POETICAL AND DRAMATIC WORKS. With Steel Plate Portrait, and an Introduction by the Author.
  Vol. II. EARLIER PAPERS—LUCK OF ROARING CAMP, and other Sketches—BOHEMIAN PAPERS—SPANISH AND AMERICAN LEGENDS.
  Vol. III. TALES OF THE ARGONAUTS—EASTERN SKETCHES.
  Vol. IV. GABRIEL CONROY.
  Vol. V. STORIES—CONDENSED NOVELS, &c.

The Select Works of Bret Harte, in Prose and Poetry. With Introductory Essay by J. M. BELLEW, Portrait of the Author, and 50 Illustrations. Crown 8vo, cloth extra, 7s. 6d.

Gabriel Conroy: A Novel. By BRET HARTE. Post 8vo, illustrated boards, 2s.

An Heiress of Red Dog, and other Stories. By BRET HARTE. Post 8vo, illustrated boards, 2s.; cloth limp, 2s. 6d.

The Twins of Table Mountain. By BRET HARTE. Fcap. 8vo, picture cover, 1s.; crown 8vo, cloth extra, 3s. 6d.

The Luck of Roaring Camp, and other Sketches. By BRET HARTE. Post 8vo, illustrated boards, 2s.

Jeff Briggs's Love Story. By BRET HARTE. Fcap. 8vo, picture cover, 1s.; cloth extra, 2s. 6d.

Flip. By BRET HARTE. Post 8vo, illustrated boards, 2s.; cloth limp, 2s. 6d.

Buchanan's (Robert) Works:

Ballads of Life, Love, and Humour. With a Frontispiece by ARTHUR HUGHES. Crown 8vo, cloth extra, 6s.

Selected Poems of Robert Buchanan. With Frontispiece by THOS. DALZIEL. Crown 8vo, cloth extra, 6s.

The Book of Orm. Crown 8vo, cloth extra, 6s.

Idyls and Legends of Inverburn. Crown 8vo, cloth extra, 6s.

St. Abe and his Seven Wives: A Tale of Salt Lake City. With a Frontispiece by A. B. HOUGHTON. Crown 8vo, cloth extra, 5s.

White Rose and Red: A Love Story. Crown 8vo, cloth extra, 6s.

The Hebrid Isles: Wanderings in the Land of Lorne and the Outer Hebrides. With Frontispiece by W. SMALL. Crown 8vo, cloth extra, 6s.

*** *See also Novels, pp.* 19 *and* 21.

Demy 8vo, cloth extra, 7s. 6d.

Burton's Anatomy of Melancholy.

A New Edition, Complete, corrected and enriched by Translations of the Classical Extracts.

*** *Also an Abridgment in "The Mayfair Library," under the title "Melancholy Anatomised," post 8vo, cloth limp,* 2s. 6d.

Burton (Captain), Works by:

The Book of the Sword: Being a History of the Sword and its Use in all Countries, from the Earliest Times. By RICHARD F. BURTON. With over 400 Illustrations. Crown 8vo, cloth extra, 25s. [*In preparation.*

To the Gold Coast for Gold: A Personal Narrative. By RICHARD F. BURTON and VERNEY LOVETT CAMERON. With Maps and Frontispiece. Two Vols., crown 8vo, 21s. [*Shortly.*

Crown 8vo, cloth extra, gilt, with Illustrations, 7s. 6d.
Byron's Letters and Journals.
With Notices of his Life. By THOMAS MOORE. A Reprint of the Original Edition, newly revised, with Twelve full-page Plates.

Two Vols., crown 8vo, cloth extra, 21s.
Cameron (Commander) and Captain Burton.
To the Gold Coast for Gold: A Personal Narrative. By RICHARD F. BURTON and VERNEY LOVETT CAMERON. With Frontispiece and Maps. [*In the press.*

Demy 8vo, cloth extra, 14s.
Campbell.—White and Black:
Travels in the United States. By Sir GEORGE CAMPBELL, M.P.

Demy 8vo, cloth extra, with Illustrations, 7s. 6d.
Caravan Route (The) between Egypt and
Syria. By His Imperial and Royal Highness the ARCHDUKE LUDWIG SALVATOR of AUSTRIA. With 23 full-page Illustrations by the Author.

Carlyle (Thomas):
Thomas Carlyle: Letters and Recollections. By MONCURE D. CONWAY, M.A. Crown 8vo, cloth extra, with Illustrations, 6s.

On the Choice of Books. With a Life of the Author by R. H. SHEPHERD. New and Revised Edition, post 8vo, cloth extra, Illustrated, 1s. 6d.

The Correspondence of Thomas Carlyle and Ralph Waldo Emerson, 1834 to 1872. Edited by CHARLES ELIOT NORTON. Two Vols. crown 8vo, cloth extra. [*Shortly.*

These letters, extending over a period of nearly forty years, were, by the common consent and direction of the illustrious writers, long since placed in Mr. Norton's hands with the fullest powers for editing and publication. It is not too much to claim that the correspondence will be found to form the most valuable and entertaining work of the kind ever issued.

Crown 8vo, cloth extra, 7s. 6d.
Century (A) of Dishonour:
A Sketch of the United States Government's Dealings with some of the Indian Tribes.

Large 4to, half-bound, profusely Illustrated, 28s.
Chatto and Jackson.—A Treatise on Wood
Engraving; Historical and Practical. By WILLIAM ANDREW CHATTO and JOHN JACKSON. With an Additional Chapter by HENRY G. BOHN; and 450 fine Illustrations. A reprint of the last Revised Edition.

Chaucer:
Chaucer for Children: A Golden Key. By Mrs. H. R. HAWEIS. With Eight Coloured Pictures and numerous Woodcuts by the Author. New Edition, small 4to, cloth extra, 6s.

Chaucer for Schools. By Mrs. H. R. HAWEIS. Demy 8vo, cloth limp, 2s. 6d.

Colman's Humorous Works:
Crown 8vo, cloth extra, gilt, 7s. 6d.
"Broad Grins," " My Nightgown and Slippers," and other Humorous Works, Prose and Poetical, of GEORGE COLMAN. With Life by G. B. BUCKSTONE, and Frontispiece by HOGARTH.

Convalescent Cookery:
Post 8vo, cloth limp, 2s. 6d.
A Family Handbook. By CATHERINE RYAN.
"*Full of sound sense and useful hints.*"—SATURDAY REVIEW.

Conway (Moncure D.), Works by:
Demonology and Devil-Lore. By MONCURE D. CONWAY, M.A. Two Vols., royal 8vo, with 65 Illustrations, 28s.
A Necklace of Stories. By MONCURE D. CONWAY, M.A. Illustrated by W. J. HENNESSY. Square 8vo, cloth extra, 6s.
The Wandering Jew. By MONCURE D. CONWAY, M.A. Crown 8vo, cloth extra, 6s.
Thomas Carlyle: Letters and Recollections. By MONCURE D. CONWAY, M.A. With Illustrations. Crown 8vo, cloth extra, 6s.

Cook (Dutton).—Hours with the Players.
New and Cheaper Edition, crown 8vo, cloth extra, 6s.
By DUTTON COOK. With a Steel Plate Frontispiece.

Copyright.—A Handbook of English and
Post 8vo, cloth limp, 2s. 6d.
Foreign Copyright in Literary and Dramatic Works. By SIDNEY JERROLD, of the Middle Temple, Esq., Barrister-at-Law.
"*Till the time arrives when copyright shall be so simple and so uniform that it can be generally understood and enjoyed, such a handbook as this will prove of great value. It is correct as well as concise, and gives just the kind and quantity of information desired by persons who are ignorant of the subject, and turn to it for information and guidance.*"—ATHENÆUM.

Cornwall.—Popular Romances of the West
Crown 8vo, cloth extra, 7s. 6d.
of England; or, The Drolls, Traditions, and Superstitions of Old Cornwall. Collected and Edited by ROBERT HUNT, F.R.S. New and Revised Edition, with Additions, and Two Steel-plate Illustrations by GEORGE CRUIKSHANK.

Creasy's Memoirs of Eminent Etonians;
Crown 8vo, cloth extra, gilt, with 13 Portraits, 7s. 6d.
With Notices of the Early History of Eton College. By Sir EDWARD CREASY, Author of "The Fifteen Decisive Battles of the World."

Credulities, Past and Present.
Crown 8vo, cloth extra, with Etched Frontispiece, 7s. 6d.
By WILLIAM JONES, F.S.A., Author of "Finger-Ring Lore," &c.

Crimes and Punishments.
Crown 8vo, cloth extra, 6s.
Including a New Translation of Beccaria's "De Delitti e delle Pene." By JAMES ANSON FARRER.

Cruikshank, George:

The Comic Almanack. Complete in TWO SERIES: The FIRST from 1835 to 1843; the SECOND from 1844 to 1853. A Gathering of the BEST HUMOUR of THACKERAY, HOOD, MAYHEW, ALBERT SMITH, A'BECKETT, ROBERT BROUGH, &c. With 2,000 Woodcuts and Steel Engravings by CRUIKSHANK, HINE, LANDELLS, &c. Crown 8vo, cloth gilt, two very thick volumes, 7s. 6d. each.

The Life of George Cruikshank. By BLANCHARD JERROLD, Author of "The Life of Napoleon III.," &c. With numerous Illustrations and a List of his Works. Two Vols., crown 8vo, cloth extra, 24s.

Crown 8vo, cloth extra, 7s. 6d.

Cussans.—Handbook of Heraldry;

with Instructions for Tracing Pedigrees and Deciphering Ancient MSS., &c. By JOHN E. CUSSANS. Entirely New and Revised Edition. Illustrated with over 400 Woodcuts and Coloured Plates.

Post 8vo, cloth limp, 2s. 6d.

Davenant.—What shall my Son be?

Hints for Parents on the Choice of a Profession or Trade for their Sons. By FRANCIS DAVENANT, M.A.

New and Cheaper Edition, crown 8vo, cloth extra, Illustrated, 7s. 6d.

Doran.—Memories of our Great Towns.

With Anecdotic Gleanings concerning their Worthies and their Oddities. By Dr. JOHN DORAN, F.S.A. With 38 Illustrations.

Crown 8vo, half-bound, 12s. 6d.

Drama, A Dictionary of the.

Being a comprehensive Guide to the Plays, Playwrights, Players, and Playhouses of the United Kingdom and America, from the Earliest to the Present Times. By W. DAVENPORT ADAMS. (Uniform with BREWER'S "Reader's Handbook.") [In preparation.

Crown 8vo, cloth extra, 6s.

Dyer.—The Folk-Lore of Plants.

By T. F. THISELTON DYER, M.A. [In preparation.

Crown 8vo, cloth boards, 6s. per Volume.

Early English Poets.

Edited, with Introductions and Annotations, by Rev. A. B. GROSART.

1. **Fletcher's (Giles, B.D.) Complete Poems**: Christ's Victorie in Heaven, Christ's Victorie on Earth, Christ's Triumph over Death, and Minor Poems. With Memorial-Introduction and Notes. One Vol.

2. **Davies' (Sir John) Complete Poetical Works**, including Psalms I. to L. in Verse, and other hitherto Unpublished MSS., for the first time Collected and Edited. With Memorial-Introduction and Notes. Two Vols.

3. **Herrick's (Robert) Hesperides**, Noble Numbers, and Complete Collected Poems. With Memorial-Introduction and Notes, Steel Portrait, Index of First Lines, and Glossarial Index, &c. Three Vols.

4. **Sidney's (Sir Philip) Complete Poetical Works**, including all those in "Arcadia." With Portrait, Memorial-Introduction, Essay on the Poetry of Sidney, and Notes. Three Vols.

Crown 8vo, cloth extra, gilt, with Illustrations, 6s.

Emanuel.—On Diamonds and Precious
Stones; their History, Value, and Properties; with Simple Tests for ascertaining their Reality. By HARRY EMANUEL, F.R.G.S. With numerous Illustrations, Tinted and Plain.

Crown 8vo, cloth extra, with Illustrations, 7s. 6d.

Englishman's House, The:
A Practical Guide to all interested in Selecting or Building a House, with full Estimates of Cost, Quantities, &c. By C. J. RICHARDSON. Third Edition. With nearly 600 Illustrations.

New and Cheaper Edition, crown 8vo cloth extra, 6s.

Ewald.—Stories from the State Papers.
By ALEX. CHARLES EWALD, F.S.A., Author of 'The Life of Prince Charles Stuart," &c. With an Autotype Facsimile.

Crown 8vo, cloth extra, with Illustrations, 6s.

Fairholt.—Tobacco :
Its History and Associations; with an Account of the Plant and its Manufacture, and its Modes of Use in all Ages and Countries. By F. W. FAIRHOLT, F.S.A. With Coloured Frontispiece and upwards of 100 Illustrations by the Author.

Demy 8vo, cloth extra, 7s. 6d.

Familiar Allusions:
A Handbook of Miscellaneous Information; including the Names of Celebrated Statues, Paintings, Palaces, Country Seats, Ruins, Churches, Ships, Streets, Clubs, Natural Curiosities, and the like. By WILLIAM A. WHEELER, Author of " Noted Names of Fiction;" and CHARLES G. WHEELER.

Faraday (Michael), Works by:
The Chemical History of a Candle: Lectures delivered before a Juvenile Audience at the Royal Institution. Edited by WILLIAM CROOKES, F.C.S. Post 8vo, cloth extra, with numerous Illustrations, 4s. 6d.

On the Various Forces of Nature, and their Relations to each other: Lectures delivered before a Juvenile Audience at the Royal Institution. Edited by WILLIAM CROOKES, F.C.S. Post 8vo, cloth extra, with numerous Illustrations, 4s. 6d.

Crown 8vo, cloth extra, with Illustrations, 7s. 6d.

Finger-Ring Lore:
Historical, Legendary, and Anecdotal. By WM. JONES, F.S.A. With Hundreds of Illustrations of Curious Rings of all Ages and Countries.
" *One of those gossiping books which are as full of amusement as of instruction.*"
—ATHENÆUM.

New and Cheaper Edition, crown 8vo, cloth extra, 6s.

Fitzgerald.—Recreations of a Literary Man;
or, Does Writing Pay? With Recollections of some Literary Men, and a View of a Literary Man's Working Life. By PERCY FITZ-GERALD.

Gardening Books:

A Year's Work in Garden and Greenhouse: Practical Advice to Amateur Gardeners as to the Management of the Flower, Fruit, and Frame Garden. By GEORGE GLENNY. Post 8vo, cloth limp, 2s. 6d.

Our Kitchen Garden: The Plants we Grow, and How we Cook Them. By TOM JERROLD, Author of "The Garden that Paid the Rent," &c. Post 8vo, cloth limp, 2s. 6d.

Household Horticulture: A Gossip about Flowers. By TOM and JANE JERROLD. Illustrated. Post 8vo, cloth limp, 2s. 6d.

The Garden that Paid the Rent. By TOM JERROLD. Fcap. 8vo, illustrated cover, 1s.; cloth limp, 1s. 6d.

My Garden Wild, and What I Grew there. By FRANCIS GEORGE HEATH. Crown 8vo, cloth extra, 5s.

One Shilling Monthly.

Gentleman's Magazine (The) for 1882.

The JANUARY Number of this Periodical contained the First Chapters of a New Serial Story, entitled "**Dust,**" by JULIAN HAWTHORNE, Author of "Garth," &c. "**Science Notes,**" by W. MATTIEU WILLIAMS, F.R.A.S., will also be continued monthly.—In JANUARY, 1883, will be begun a New Serial Novel by ROBERT BUCHANAN, entitled "**The New Abelard.**"

⁎ Now ready, the Volume for JANUARY to JUNE, 1882, cloth extra, price 8s. 6d; and Cases for binding, price 2s. each.

Gentleman's Annual (The).

Containing Two Complete Novels by R. E. FRANCILLON and the Author of "Miss Molly." Demy 8vo, illuminated cover, 1s.

THE RUSKIN GRIMM.—Square 8vo, cl. ex., 6s. 6d.; gilt edges, 7s. 6d.

German Popular Stories.

Collected by the Brothers GRIMM, and Translated by EDGAR TAYLOR. Edited with an Introduction by JOHN RUSKIN. With 22 Illustrations on Steel by GEORGE CRUIKSHANK. Both Series Complete.

"*The illustrations of this volume . . . are of quite sterling and admirable art, of a class precisely parallel in elevation to the character of the tales which they illustrate; and the original etchings, as I have before said in the Appendix to my 'Elements of Drawing,' were unrivalled in masterfulness of touch since Rembrandt (in some qualities of delineation, unrivalled even by him). . . . To make somewhat enlarged copies of them, looking at them through a magnifying glass, and never putting two lines where Cruikshank has put only one, would be an exercise in decision and severe drawing which would leave afterwards little to be learnt in schools.*"—Extract from Introduction by JOHN RUSKIN.

Post 8vo, cloth limp, 2s. 6d.

Glenny.—A Year's Work in Garden and

Greenhouse: Practical Advice to Amateur Gardeners as to the Management of the Flower, Fruit, and Frame Garden. By GEORGE GLENNY.

"*A great deal of valuable information, conveyed in very simple language. The amateur need not wish for a better guide.*"—LEEDS MERCURY.

Crown 8vo, cloth gilt and gilt edges, 7s. 6d.

Golden Treasury of Thought, The:

An ENCYCLOPÆDIA OF QUOTATIONS from Writers of all Times and Countries. Selected and Edited by THEODORE TAYLOR.

Golden Library, The:

Square 16mo (Tauchnitz size), cloth extra, 2s. per volume.

Ballad History of England. By W. C. BENNETT.

Bayard Taylor's Diversions of the Echo Club.

Byron's Don Juan.

Emerson's Letters and Social Aims.

Godwin's (William) Lives of the Necromancers.

Holmes's Autocrat of the Breakfast Table. With an Introduction by G. A. SALA.

Holmes's Professor at the Breakfast Table.

Hood's Whims and Oddities. Complete. With all the original Illustrations.

Irving's (Washington) Tales of a Traveller.

Irving's (Washington) Tales of the Alhambra.

Jesse's (Edward) Scenes and Occupations of Country Life.

Lamb's Essays of Elia. Both Series Complete in One Vol.

Leigh Hunt's Essays: A Tale for a Chimney Corner, and other Pieces. With Portrait, and Introduction by EDMUND OLLIER.

Mallory's (Sir Thomas) Mort d'Arthur: The Stories of King Arthur and of the Knights of the Round Table. Edited by B. MONTGOMERIE RANKING.

Pascal's Provincial Letters. A New Translation, with Historical Introduction and Notes, by T. M'CRIE, D.D.

Pope's Poetical Works. Complete.

Rochefoucauld's Maxims and Moral Reflections. With Notes, and an Introductory Essay by SAINTE-BEUVE.

St. Pierre's Paul and Virginia, and The Indian Cottage. Edited, with Life, by the Rev. E. CLARKE.

Shelley's Early Poems, and Queen Mab, with Essay by LEIGH HUNT.

Shelley's Later Poems: Laon and Cythna, &c.

Shelley's Posthumous Poems, the Shelley Papers, &c.

Shelley's Prose Works, including A Refutation of Deism, Zastrozzi, St. Irvyne, &c.

White's Natural History of Selborne. Edited, with Additions, by THOMAS BROWN, F.L.S.

New and Cheaper Edition, demy 8vo, cloth extra, with Illustrations, 7s. 6d.

Greeks and Romans, The Life of the,
Described from Antique Monuments. By ERNST GUHL and W. KONER. Translated from the Third German Edition, and Edited by Dr. F. HUEFFER. With 545 Illustrations.

"*Must find a place, not only upon the scholar's shelves, but in every well-chosen library of art.*"—DAILY NEWS.

Crown 8vo, cloth extra, gilt, with Illustrations, 4s. 6d.

Guyot.—The Earth and Man;
or, Physical Geography in its relation to the History of Mankind. By ARNOLD GUYOT. With Additions by Professors AGASSIZ, PIERCE, and GRAY; 12 Maps and Engravings on Steel, some Coloured, and copious Index.

Crown 8vo, 1s.; cloth, 1s. 6d.

Hair (The): Its Treatment in Health, Weakness, and Disease. Translated from the German of Dr. J. PINCUS.

Hake (Dr. Thomas Gordon), Poems by:
Maiden Ecstasy. Small 4to, cloth extra, 8s.
New Symbols. Crown 8vo, cloth extra, 6s.
Legends of the Morrow. Crown 8vo, cloth extra, 6s.
The Serpent Play. Crown 8vo, cloth extra, 6s. [*Shortly*

Two Vols., crown 8vo, cloth extra, 12s.
Half-Hours with Foreign Novelists.
With Notices of their Lives and Writings. By HELEN and ALICE ZIMMERN. A New Edition.

Medium 8vo, cloth extra, gilt, with Illustrations, 7s. 6d.
Hall.—Sketches of Irish Character. By Mrs.
S. C. HALL. With numerous Illustrations on Steel and Wood by MACLISE, GILBERT, HARVEY, and G. CRUIKSHANK.

"*The Irish Sketches of this lady resemble Miss Mitford's beautiful English sketches in 'Our Village,' but they are far more vigorous and picturesque and bright.*"—BLACKWOOD'S MAGAZINE.

Haweis (Mrs.), Works by:
The Art of Dress. By Mrs. H. R. HAWEIS. Illustrated by the Author. Small 8vo, illustrated cover, 1s.; cloth limp, 1s. 6d.

"*A well-considered attempt to apply canons of good taste to the costumes of ladies of our time. . . . Mrs. Haweis writes frankly and to the point; she does not mince matters, but boldly remonstrates with her own sex on the follies they indulge in. . . . We may recommend the book to the ladies whom it concerns.*"—ATHENÆUM.

The Art of Beauty. By Mrs. H. R. HAWEIS. Square 8vo, cloth extra, gilt, gilt edges, with Coloured Frontispiece and nearly 100 Illustrations, 10s. 6d.

The Art of Decoration. By Mrs. H. R. HAWEIS. Square 8vo, handsomely bound and profusely Illustrated, 10s. 6d.

* See also CHAUCER, *p. 6 of this Catalogue.*

Crown 8vo, cloth extra, 6s.
Haweis (Rev. H. R.).—American Humorists.
Including WASHINGTON IRVING, OLIVER WENDELL HOLMES, JAMES RUSSELL LOWELL, ARTEMUS WARD, MARK TWAIN, and BRET HARTE. By the Rev. H. R. HAWEIS, M.A. [*Shortly.*

Crown 8vo, cloth extra, 5s.
Heath (F. G.)—My Garden Wild,
And What I Grew there. By FRANCIS GEORGE HEATH, Author of "The Fern World," &c.

"*If gardens of wild flowers do not begin at once to spring up over half the little patches of back yard within fifty miles of London it will not be Mr. Heath's fault, for a more exquisite picture of the felicity of horticulture has seldom been drawn for us by so charming and graphic a word-painter as the writer of this pleasant little volume.*"—GRANT ALLEN, in THE ACADEMY.

SPECIMENS OF MODERN POETS.—Crown 8vo, cloth extra, 6s.
Heptalogia (The); or, The Seven against Sense.
A Cap with Seven Bells.

"*The merits of the book cannot be fairly estimated by means of a few extracts; should be read at length to be appreciated properly, and in our opinion its merits entitle it to be very widely read indeed.*"—ST. JAMES'S GAZETTE.

Cr. 8vo, bound in parchment, 8s.; Large-Paper copies (only 50 printed), 15s.
Herbert.—The Poems of Lord Herbert of
Cherbury. Edited, with an Introduction, by J. CHURTON COLLINS.

Crown 8vo, cloth limp, with Illustrations, 2s. 6d.
Holmes.—The Science of Voice Production
and Voice Preservation : A Popular Manual for the Use of Speakers and Singers. By GORDON HOLMES, M.D.

"*The advice the author gives, coming as it does from one having authority, is most valuable.*"—NATURE.

Crown 8vo, cloth extra, gilt, 7s. 6d.
Hood's (Thomas) Choice Works,
In Prose and Verse. Including the CREAM OF THE COMIC ANNUALS. With Life of the Author, Portrait, and Two Hundred Illustrations.

Square crown 8vo, cloth extra, gilt edges, 6s.
Hood's (Tom) From Nowhere to the North
Pole: A Noah's Arkæological Narrative. With 25 Illustrations by W. BRUNTON and E. C. BARNES.

Crown 8vo, cloth extra, gilt, 7s. 6d.
Hook's (Theodore) Choice Humorous Works,
including his Ludicrous Adventures, Bons-mots, Puns and Hoaxes. With a new Life of the Author, Portraits, Facsimiles and Illustrations.

Tenth Edition, crown 8vo, cloth extra, 7s.
Horne.—Orion :
An Epic Poem, in Three Books. By RICHARD HENGIST HORNE. With Photographic Portrait from a Medallion by SUMMERS.

Crown 8vo, cloth extra, 7s. 6d.
Howell.—Conflicts of Capital and Labour
Historically and Economically considered. Being a History and Review of the Trade Unions of Great Britain, showing their Origin, Progress, Constitution, and Objects, in their Political, Social, Economical, and Industrial Aspects. By GEORGE HOWELL.

"*This book is an attempt, and on the whole a successful attempt, to place the work of trade unions in the past, and their objects in the future, fairly before the public from the working man's point of view.*"—PALL MALL GAZETTE.

Demy 8vo, cloth extra, 12s. 6d.
Hueffer.—The Troubadours :
A History of Provençal Life and Literature in the Middle Ages. By FRANCIS HUEFFER.

Crown 8vo, cloth extra, 6s.
Ireland under the Land Act :
Letters to the *Standard* during the Crisis. Containing the most recent Information about the State of the Country, the Popular Leaders, the League, the Working of the Sub-Commissions, &c. With Leading Cases under the Act, giving the Evidence in full; Judicial Dicta, &c. By E. CANT-WALL.

Crown 8vo, cloth extra, 6s.
Janvier.—Practical Keramics for Students.
By CATHERINE A. JANVIER.

"*Will be found a useful handbook by those who wish to try the manufacture or decoration of pottery, and may be studied by all who desire to know something of the art.*"—MORNING POST.

A New Edition, crown 8vo, cloth extra, Illustrated, 7s. 6d.

Jennings.—The Rosicrucians:
Their Rites and Mysteries. With Chapters on the Ancient Fire and Serpent Worshippers. By HARGRAVE JENNINGS. With Five full page Plates and upwards of 300 Illustrations.

Jerrold (Tom), Works by:
The Garden that Paid the Rent. By TOM JERROLD. Fcap. 8vo, illustrated cover, 1s.; cloth limp, 1s. 6d

Household Horticulture: A Gossip about Flowers. By TOM and JANE JERROLD. Illustrated. Post 8vo, cloth limp, 2s. 6d.

Our Kitchen Garden: The Plants we Grow, and How we Cook Them. By TOM JERROLD, Author of "The Garden that Paid the Rent," &c. Post 8vo, cloth limp, 2s. 6d.

"*The combination of hints on cookery with gardening has been very cleverly carried out, and the result is an interesting and highly instructive little work. Mr. Jerrold is correct in saying that English people do not make half the use of vegetables they might; and by showing how easily they can be grown, and so obtained fresh, he is doing a great deal to make them more popular.*"—DAILY CHRONICLE.

Two Vols. 8vo, with 52 Illustrations and Maps, cloth extra, gilt, 14s.

Josephus, The Complete Works of.
Translated by WHISTON. Containing both "The Antiquities of the Jews" and "The Wars of the Jews."

Small 8vo, cloth, full gilt, gilt edges, with Illustrations, 6s.

Kavanagh.—The Pearl Fountain,
And other Fairy Stories. By BRIDGET and JULIA KAVANAGH. With Thirty Illustrations by J. MOYR SMITH.

"*Genuine new fairy stories of the old type, some of them as delightful as the best of Grimm's 'German Popular Stories.' . . . For the most part the stories are downright, thorough-going fairy stories of the most admirable kind. . . . Mr. Moyr Smith's illustrations, too, are admirable.*"—SPECTATOR.

Square 8vo, cloth extra, with Illustrations, 6s.

Knight (The) and the Dwarf.
By CHARLES MILLS. With Illustrations by THOMAS LINDSAY.

Crown 8vo, illustrated boards, with numerous Plates, 2s. 6d.

Lace (Old Point), and How to Copy and
Imitate it. By DAISY WATERHOUSE HAWKINS. With 17 Illustrations by the Author.

Lane's Arabian Nights, &c.:
The Thousand and One Nights: Commonly called, in England, "THE ARABIAN NIGHTS' ENTERTAINMENTS." A New Translation from the Arabic, with copious Notes, by EDWARD WILLIAM LANE. Illustrated by many hundred Engravings on Wood, from Original Designs by WILLIAM HARVEY. A New Edition, from a Copy annotated by the Translator, edited by his Nephew, EDWARD STANLEY POOLE. With a Preface by STANLEY LANE-POOLE. Three Vols., demy 8vo, cloth extra, 7s. 6d. each.

Arabian Society in the Middle Ages: Stories from "The Thousand and One Nights." By EDWARD WILLIAM LANE, Author of "The Modern Egyptians," &c. Edited by STANLEY LANE-POOLE. Crown 8vo, cloth extra, 6s. [*In the press*

Lamb (Charles):

Mary and Charles Lamb: Their Poems, Letters, and Remains. With Reminiscences and Notes by W. CAREW HAZLITT. With HANCOCK'S Portrait of the Essayist, Facsimiles of the Title-pages of the rare First Editions of Lamb's and Coleridge's Works, and numerous Illustrations. Crown 8vo, cloth extra, 10s. 6d.

Lamb's Complete Works, in Prose and Verse, reprinted from the Original Editions, with many Pieces hitherto unpublished. Edited, with Notes and Introduction, by R. H. SHEPHERD. With Two Portraits and Facsimile of a Page of the "Essay on Roast Pig." Crown 8vo, cloth extra, 7s. 6d.

"*A complete edition of Lamb's writings, in prose and verse, has long been wanted, and is now supplied. The editor appears to have taken great pains to bring together Lamb's scattered contributions, and his collection contains a number of pieces which are now reproduced for the first time since their original appearance in various old periodicals.*"—SATURDAY REVIEW.

Poetry for Children, and Prince Dorus. By CHARLES LAMB. Carefully Reprinted from unique copies. Small 8vo, cloth extra, 5s.

"*The quaint and delightful little book, over the recovery of which all the hearts of his lovers are yet warm with rejoicing.*"—A. C. SWINBURNE.

Crown 8vo, cloth extra, 6s.

Lares and Penates;

Or, The Background of Life. By FLORENCE CADDY.

"*The whole book is well worth reading, for it is full of practical suggestions. We hope nobody will be deterred from taking up a book which teaches a good deal about sweetening poor lives as well as giving grace to wealthy ones.*"—GRAPHIC.

Crown 8vo, cloth extra, with Illustrations, 7s. 6d.

Life in London;

or, The History of Jerry Hawthorn and Corinthian Tom. With the whole of CRUIKSHANK'S Illustrations, in Colours, after the Originals.

Crown 8vo, cloth extra, 6s.

Lights on the Way:

Some Tales within a Tale. By the late J H. ALEXANDER, B.A. Edited, with an Explanatory Note, by H. A. PAGE, Author of "Thoreau: A Study."

Longfellow:

Longfellow's Complete Prose Works. Including "Outre Mer," "Hyperion," "Kavanagh," "The Poets and Poetry of Europe," and "Driftwood." With Portrait and Illustrations by VALENTINE BROMLEY. Crown 8vo, cloth extra, 7s. 6d.

Longfellow's Poetical Works. Carefully Reprinted from the Original Editions. With numerous fine Illustrations on Steel and Wood. Crown 8vo, cloth extra, 7s. 6d.

Crown 8vo, cloth extra, 5s.

Lunatic Asylum, My Experiences in a.

By A SANE PATIENT.

"*The story is clever and interesting, sad beyond measure though the subject be. There is no personal bitterness, and no violence or anger. Whatever may have been the evidence for our author's madness when he was consigned to an asylum, nothing can be clearer than his sanity when he wrote this book; it is bright, calm, and to the point.*"—SPECTATOR.

Demy 8vo, with Fourteen full-page Plates, cloth boards, 18s.

Lusiad (The) of Camoens.
Translated into English Spenserian Verse by ROBERT FFRENCH DUFF.

McCarthy (Justin), Works by:
History of Our Own Times, from the Accession of Queen Victoria to the General Election of 1880. By JUSTIN MCCARTHY, M.P. Four Vols., demy 8vo, cloth extra, 12s. each.—Also a POPULAR EDITION, in Four Vols., crown 8vo, cloth extra, 6s. each.

"*Criticism is disarmed before a composition which provokes little but approval. This is a really good book on a really interesting subject, and words piled on words could say no more for it.*"—SATURDAY REVIEW.

History of the Four Georges. By JUSTIN MCCARTHY, M.P. Four Vols. demy 8vo, cloth extra, 12s. each. [*In preparation.*

* For *Mr. McCarthy's Novels, see pp.* 22, 24.

Small crown 8vo, cloth extra, 5s.

MacDonald (George).—The Princess and
Curdie. By GEORGE MACDONALD, LL.D. With 11 Illustrations by JAMES ALLEN.

Crown 8vo, cloth extra, 7s. 6d.

Maclise Gallery (The) of Illustrious Literary
Characters: 85 fine Portraits, with Descriptive Text, Anecdotal and Biographical, by WILLIAM BATES, B.A. [*In preparation.*

Macquoid (Mrs.), Works by:
In the Ardennes. By KATHARINE S. MACQUOID. With 50 fine Illustrations by THOMAS R. MACQUOID. Square 8vo, cloth extra, 10s. 6d.

Pictures and Legends from Normandy and Brittany. By KATHARINE S. MACQUOID. With numerous Illustrations by THOMAS R. MACQUOID. Square 8vo, cloth gilt, 10s. 6d.

Through Normandy. By KATHARINE S. MACQUOID. With 90 Illustrations by T. R. MACQUOID. Square 8vo, cloth extra, 7s. 6d.

Through Brittany. By KATHARINE S. MACQUOID. With numerous Illustrations by T. R. MACQUOID. Sq. 8vo, cloth extra, 7s. 6d.

About Yorkshire. By KATHARINE S. MACQUOID. With about 70 Illustrations by THOMAS R. MACQUOID, Engraved by SWAIN. Square 8vo, cloth extra, 10s. 6d. [*In preparation.*

"*The pleasant companionship which Mrs. Macquoid offers, while wandering from one point of interest to another, seems to throw a renewed charm around each oft-depicted scene.*"—MORNING POST.

Mallock (W. H.), Works by:
Is Life Worth Living? By WILLIAM HURRELL MALLOCK. Crown 8vo, cloth extra, 6s.

The New Republic; or, Culture, Faith, and Philosophy in an English Country House. By W. H. MALLOCK. Post 8vo, cloth limp, 2s. 6d.

The New Paul and Virginia; or, Positivism on an Island. By W. H. MALLOCK. Post 8vo, cloth limp, 2s. 6d.

Poems. By W. H. MALLOCK. Small 4to, bound in parchment, 8s.

A Romance of the Nineteenth Century. By W. H. MALLOCK. Second Edition, with a Preface. Two Vols., crown 8vo, 21s.

Handsomely printed in facsimile, price 5s.

Magna Charta.

An exact Facsimile of the Original Document in the British Museum, printed on fine plate paper, nearly 3 feet long by 2 feet wide, with the Arms and Seals emblazoned in Gold and Colours.

Mark Twain, Works by:

The Choice Works of Mark Twain. Revised and Corrected throughout by the Author. With Life, Portrait, and numerous Illustrations. Crown 8vo, cloth extra, 7s. 6d.

The Adventures of Tom Sawyer. By MARK TWAIN. With 100 Illustrations. Small 8vo, cloth extra, 7s. 6d. CHEAP EDITION, illust. bds., 2s.

A Pleasure Trip on the Continent of Europe: The Innocents Abroad, and The New Pilgrim's Progress. By MARK TWAIN. Post 8vo, illustrated boards, 2s.

An Idle Excursion, and other Sketches. By MARK TWAIN. Post 8vo, illustrated boards, 2s.

The Prince and the Pauper. By MARK TWAIN. With nearly 200 Illustrations. Crown 8vo, cloth extra, 7s. 6d.

The Innocents Abroad; or, The New Pilgrim's Progress: Being some Account of the Steamship "Quaker City's" Pleasure Excursion to Europe and the Holy Land. With 234 Illustrations. By MARK TWAIN. Crown 8vo, cloth extra, 7s. 6d.

The Innocents at Home; and Roughing It. By MARK TWAIN. With 200 Illustrations by F. A. FRASER. Crown 8vo, cloth extra, 7s. 6d.

The Stolen White Elephant, &c. By MARK TWAIN. Crown 8vo, cloth extra, 6s.

Mississippi Sketches. By MARK TWAIN. With about 300 Original Illustrations. Crown 8vo, cloth extra, 7s. 6d. [*In preparation.*

A Tramp Abroad. By MARK TWAIN. With 314 Illustrations. Crown 8vo, cloth extra, 7s. 6d.

"*The fun and tenderness of the conception, of which no living man but Mark Twain is capable, its grace and fantasy and slyness, the wonderful feeling for animals that is manifest in every line, make of all this episode of Jim Baker and his jays a piece of work that is not only delightful as mere reading, but also of a high degree of merit as literature. . . . The book is full of good things, and contains passages and episodes that are equal to the funniest of those that have gone before.*"—ATHENÆUM.

Small 8vo, cloth limp, with Illustrations, 2s. 6d.

Miller.—Physiology for the Young;

Or, The House of Life: Human Physiology, with its application to the Preservation of Health. For use in Classes and Popular Reading. With numerous Illustrations. By Mrs. F. FENWICK MILLER.

"*An admirable introduction to a subject which all who value health and enjoy life should have at their fingers' ends.*"—ECHO.

Milton (J. L.), Works by:

The Hygiene of the Skin. A Concise Set of Rules for the Management of the Skin; with Directions for Diet, Wines, Soaps, Baths, &c. By J. L. MILTON, Senior Surgeon to St. John's Hospital. Small 8vo, 1s.; cloth extra, 1s. 6d.

The Bath in Diseases of the Skin. Small 8vo, 1s.; cloth extra, 1s. 6d.

Post 8vo, cloth limp, 2s. 6d. per volume.

Mayfair Library, The:

The New Republic. By W. H. MALLOCK.
The New Paul and Virginia. By W. H. MALLOCK.
The True History of Joshua Davidson. By E. LYNN LINTON.
Old Stories Re-told. By WALTER THORNBURY.
Thoreau: His Life and Aims. By H. A. PAGE.
By Stream and Sea. By WILLIAM SENIOR.
Jeux d'Esprit. Edited by HENRY S. LEIGH.
Puniana. By the Hon. HUGH ROWLEY.
More Puniana. By the Hon. HUGH ROWLEY.
Puck on Pegasus. By H. CHOLMONDELEY-PENNELL.
The Speeches of Charles Dickens.
Muses of Mayfair. Edited by H. CHOLMONDELEY-PENNELL.
Gastronomy as a Fine Art. By BRILLAT-SAVARIN.
The Philosophy of Handwriting. DON FELIX DE SALAMANCA.
Curiosities of Criticism. By HENRY J. JENNINGS.
Literary Frivolities, Fancies, Follies, Frolics. By W. T. DOBSON.
Poetical Ingenuities and Eccentricities. Selected and Edited by W. T. DOBSON.
Pencil and Palette. By ROBERT KEMPT.
Latter-Day Lyrics. Edited by W. DAVENPORT ADAMS.
Original Plays by W. S. GILBERT. FIRST SERIES. Containing: The Wicked World—Pygmalion and Galatea—Charity—The Princess—The Palace of Truth—Trial by Jury.
Original Plays by W. S. GILBERT. SECOND SERIES. Containing: Broken Hearts—Engaged—Sweethearts—Dan'l Druce—Gretchen—Tom Cobb—The Sorcerer—H.M.S. Pinafore—The Pirates of Penzance.
Carols of Cockayne. By HENRY S. LEIGH.
The Book of Clerical Anecdotes. By JACOB LARWOOD.
The Agony Column of "The Times," from 1800 to 1870. Edited, with an Introduction, by ALICE CLAY.
The Cupboard Papers. By FIN-BEC.
Pastimes and Players. By ROBERT MACGREGOR.
Balzac's "Comédie Humaine" and its Author. With Translations by H. H. WALKER.
Melancholy Anatomised: A Popular Abridgment of "Burton's Anatomy of Melancholy."
Quips and Quiddities. Selected by W. DAVENPORT ADAMS.
Leaves from a Naturalist's Note-Book. By Dr. ANDREW WILSON.
The Autocrat of the Breakfast-Table. By O. WENDELL HOLMES. Illustrated by J. GORDON THOMSON.
Forensic Anecdotes; or, Humour and Curiosities of the Law and Men of Law. By JACOB LARWOOD.
Theatrical Anecdotes. By JACOB LARWOOD.
Witch Stories. By E. L. LINTON.

Large 4to, bound in buckram, 21s.

Moncrieff.—The Abdication; or, Time Tries All.
An Historical Drama. By W. D. SCOTT-MONCRIEFF. With Seven Etchings by JOHN PETTIE, R.A., W. Q. ORCHARDSON, R.A., J. MAC WHIRTER, A.R.A., COLIN HUNTER, R. MACBETH. and TOM GRAHAM.

Square 8vo, cloth extra, with numerous Illustrations, 7s. 6d.

North Italian Folk.
By Mrs. COMYNS CARR. Illustrated by RANDOLPH CALDECOTT.

"*A delightful book, of a kind which is far too rare. If anyone wants to really know the North Italian folk, we can honestly advise him to omit the journey, and read Mrs. Carr's pages instead. . . Description with Mrs. Carr is a real gift. It is rarely that a book is so happily illustrated.*"—CONTEMPORARY REVIEW.

New Novels:

ALL SORTS AND CONDITIONS OF MEN: An Impossible Story. By WALTER BESANT. Illust. by FRED. BARNARD. 3 vols., cr. 8vo.

VALENTINA: A Sketch. By ELEANOR C. PRICE. 2 vols., cr. 8vo.

KEPT IN THE DARK. By ANTHONY TROLLOPE. With a Frontispiece by J. E. MILLAIS, R.A. 2 vols., post 8vo, 12s. [*Oct.* 20.

VAL STRANGE: A Story of the Primrose Way. By DAVID CHRISTIE MURRAY. 3 vols., crown 8vo. [*Shortly.*

REGIMENTAL LEGENDS. By J. S. WINTER, Author of "Cavalry Life," &c. 3 vols., crown 8vo. [*Shortly.*

THE GOLDEN SHAFT. By CHARLES GIBBON, Author of "Robin Gray," &c. 3 vols., crown 8vo. [*Shortly.*

A NEW NOVEL BY OUIDA is now in preparation, in 3 vols., crown 8vo.

FOXGLOVE MANOR. By ROBERT BUCHANAN, Author of "God and the Man," &c. 3 vols., crown 8vo. [*Shortly.*

DUST: A Story. By JULIAN HAWTHORNE, Author of "Garth," "Sebastian Strome," &c. 3 vols., crown 8vo. [*Shortly.*

A NEW NOVEL by WILKIE COLLINS is now in preparation, in 3 vols., crown 8vo.

WOMEN ARE STRANGE, and other Stories. By F. W. ROBINSON, Author of "Grandmother's Money," &c. 3 vols. [*Shortly.*

A NEW COLLECTION of STORIES by CHARLES READE is now in preparation, in 3 vols., crown 8vo.

Post 8vo, cloth extra, Illustrated, 5s.

Number Nip (Stories about),
The Spirit of the Giant Mountains. Retold for Children by WALTER GRAHAME. With Illustrations by J. MOYR SMITH.

O'Shaughnessy (Arthur), Works by:

Songs of a Worker. By ARTHUR O'SHAUGHNESSY. Fcap. 8vo, cloth extra, 7s. 6d.

Music and Moonlight. By ARTHUR O'SHAUGHNESSY. Fcap. 8vo, cloth extra, 7s. 6d.

Lays of France. By ARTHUR O'SHAUGHNESSY. Crown 8vo, cloth extra, 10s. 6d.

Crown 8vo, red cloth extra, 5s. each.

Ouida's Novels.—Library Edition.

Held in Bondage.	Pascarel.
Strathmore.	Two Little Wooden Shoes.
Chandos.	Signa.
Under Two Flags.	In a Winter City.
Idalia.	Ariadne.
Cecil Castlemaine's Gage.	Friendship.
Tricotrin.	Moths.
Puck.	Pipistrello.
Folle Farine.	A Village Commune.
A Dog of Flanders.	In Maremma.

*** Also a Cheap Edition of all but the last, post 8vo, illustrated boards, 2s. each.

OUIDA'S NEW STORIES.—Sq. 8vo, cloth gilt, cinnamon edges, 7s. 6d.

BIMBI: Stories for Children. By OUIDA.

Crown 8vo, cloth extra, with Vignette Portraits, price 6s. per Vol.

Old Dramatists, The:

Ben Jonson's Works.
With Notes Critical and Explanatory, and a Biographical Memoir by WILLIAM GIFFORD. Edited by Colonel CUNNINGHAM. Three Vols.

Chapman's Works.
Complete in Three Vols. Vol. I. contains the Plays complete, including the doubtful ones; Vol. II. the Poems and Minor Translations, with an Introductory Essay by ALGERNON CHARLES SWINBURNE; Vol. III. the Translations of the Iliad and Odyssey.

Marlowe's Works.
Including his Translations. Edited, with Notes and Introduction, by Col. CUNNINGHAM. One Vol.

Massinger's Plays.
From the Text of WILLIAM GIFFORD. Edited by Col. CUNNINGHAM. One Vol.

Post 8vo, cloth limp, 1s. 6d.

Parliamentary Procedure, A Popular Handbook of. By HENRY W. LUCY.

Crown 8vo, cloth extra, 6s.

Payn.—Some Private Views:

Being Essays contributed to *The Nineteenth Century* and to *The Times*. By JAMES PAYN, Author of "Lost Sir Massingberd," &c.

*** *For Mr. PAYN'S Novels, see pp. 22, 24, 25.*

Two Vols. 8vo, cloth extra, with Portraits, 10s. 6d.

Plutarch's Lives of Illustrious Men.

Translated from the Greek, with Notes Critical and Historical, and a Life of Plutarch, by JOHN and WILLIAM LANGHORNE.

Proctor (R. A.), Works by:

Easy Star Lessons. With Star Maps for Every Night in the Year, Drawings of the Constellations, &c. Crown 8vo, cloth extra, 6s.

Familiar Science Studies. Crown 8vo, cloth extra, 7s. 6d.

Myths and Marvels of Astronomy. By RICHARD A. PROCTOR. Crown 8vo, cloth extra, 6s.

Pleasant Ways in Science. Crown 8vo, cloth extra, 6s.

Rough Ways made Smooth: A Series of Familiar Essays on Scientific Subjects. By R. A. PROCTOR. Crown 8vo, cloth extra, 6s.

Our Place among Infinities: A Series of Essays contrasting our Little Abode in Space and Time with the Infinities Around us. By RICHARD A. PROCTOR. Crown 8vo, cloth extra, 6s.

The Expanse of Heaven: A Series of Essays on the Wonders of the Firmament. By RICHARD A. PROCTOR. Crown 8vo, cloth, 6s.

Saturn and its System. By RICHARD A. PROCTOR. New and Revised Edition, with 13 Steel Plates, demy 8vo, cloth extra, 10s. 6d.

The Great Pyramid: Its Plan and Purpose. By RICHARD A. PROCTOR. With Illustrations. Crown 8vo, cloth extra, 6s. [*Immediately.*

Mysteries of Time and Space. By RICHARD A. PROCTOR. With Illustrations. Crown 8vo, cloth extra, 7s. 6d. [*In preparation.*

Wages and Wants of Science Workers. Crown 8vo, 1s. 6d.

"*Mr. Proctor, of all writers of our time, best conforms to Matthew Arnold's conception of a man of culture, in that he strives to humanise knowledge and divest it of whatever is harsh, crude, or technical, and so makes it a source of happiness and brightness for all.*"—WESTMINSTER REVIEW.

LIBRARY EDITIONS, many Illustrated, crown 8vo, cloth extra, 3s. 6d. each.

Piccadilly Novels, The.
Popular Stories by the Best Authors.

BY MRS. ALEXANDER.
Maid, Wife, or Widow?

BY W. BESANT & JAMES RICE.
Ready-Money Mortiboy.
My Little Girl.
The Case of Mr. Lucraft.
This Son of Vulcan.
With Harp and Crown.
The Golden Butterfly.
By Celia's Arbour.
The Monks of Thelema.
'Twas in Trafalgar's Bay.
The Seamy Side.
The Ten Years' Tenant.
The Chaplain of the Fleet.

BY ROBERT BUCHANAN.
A Child of Nature.
God and the Man.

BY MRS. H. LOVETT CAMERON.
Deceivers Ever.
Juliet's Guardian.

BY WILKIE COLLINS.
Antonina.
Basil.
Hide and Seek.
The Dead Secret.
Queen of Hearts.
My Miscellanies.
The Woman in White.
The Moonstone.
Man and Wife.
Poor Miss Finch.
Miss or Mrs?
The New Magdalen.
The Frozen Deep.
The Law and the Lady.
The Two Destinies.
The Haunted Hotel.
The Fallen Leaves.
Jezebel's Daughter.
The Black Robe.

BY M. BETHAM-EDWARDS.
Felicia.

BY MRS. ANNIE EDWARDES.
Archie Lovell.

BY R. E. FRANCILLON.
Olympia.
Queen Cophetua.

BY ÉDWARD GARRETT.
The Capel Girls.

BY CHARLES GIBBON.
Robin Gray.
For Lack of Gold.
In Love and War.
What will the World Say?
For the King.
In Honour Bound.
Queen of the Meadow.
In Pastures Green.
The Flower of the Forest.
A Heart's Problem.

BY THOMAS HARDY.
Under the Greenwood Tree.

BY JULIAN HAWTHORNE.
Garth.
Ellice Quentin.
Sebastian Strome.

BY MRS ALFRED HUNT.
Thornicroft's Model.
The Leaden Casket.

BY JEAN INGELOW.
Fated to be Free.

BY HENRY JAMES, Jun.
Confidence.

BY HARRIETT JAY.
The Queen of Connaught.
The Dark Colleen.

BY HENRY KINGSLEY.
Number Seventeen.
Oakshott Castle.

BY E. LYNN LINTON.
Patricia Kemball.
Atonement of Leam Dundas.
The World Well Lost.
Under which Lord?
With a Silken Thread.
The Rebel of the Family.
"My Love!"

BOOKS PUBLISHED BY

PICCADILLY NOVELS—*continued*.

BY JUSTIN McCARTHY, M.P.
The Waterdale Neighbours.
My Enemy's Daughter.
Linley Rochford.
A Fair Saxon.
Dear Lady Disdain.
Miss Misanthrope.
Donna Quixote.
The Comet of a Season.

BY AGNES MACDONELL.
Quaker Cousins.

BY KATHARINE S. MACQUOID.
Lost Rose.
The Evil Eye.

BY FLORENCE MARRYAT.
Open! Sesame!
Written in Fire.

BY JEAN MIDDLEMASS.
Touch and Go.

BY D. CHRISTIE MURRAY.
A Life's Atonement.
Joseph's Coat.

BY MRS. OLIPHANT.
Whiteladies.

BY JAMES PAYN.
Lost Sir Massingberd.
The Best of Husbands.
Fallen Fortunes.
Halves.
Walter's Word
What He Cost Her.
Less Black than We're Painted.
By Proxy.
Under One Roof.
High Spirits.
From Exile.
Carlyon's Year.
A Confidential Agent.

BY CHARLES READE, D.C.L.
It is Never Too Late to Mend.
Hard Cash.
Peg Woffington.
Christie Johnstone.
Griffith Gaunt.
The Double Marriage.
Love Me Little, Love Me Long.
Foul Play.
The Cloister and the Hearth.
The Course of True Love.
The Autobiography of a Thief.
Put Yourself in His Place.
A Terrible Temptation.
The Wandering Heir.
A Simpleton.
A Woman-Hater.
Readiana.

BY MRS. J. H. RIDDELL.
Her Mother's Darling.

BY JOHN SAUNDERS.
Bound to the Wheel.
Guy Waterman.
One Against the World.
The Lion in the Path.
The Two Dreamers.

BY BERTHA THOMAS.
Proud Maisie.
Cressida.
The Violin-Player.

BY ANTHONY TROLLOPE.
The Way we Live Now.
The American Senator.

BY T. A. TROLLOPE.
Diamond Cut Diamond.

BY SARAH TYTLER.
What She Came Through.
The Bride's Pass.

BY J. S. WINTER.
Cavalry Life.

NEW VOLUMES OF THE PICCADILLY NOVELS.

A Grape from a Thorn. By JAMES PAYN. Illustrated by W. SMALL.
Frau Frohmann. By ANTHONY TROLLOPE. With Frontispiece by H. FRENCH.
For Cash Only. By JAMES PAYN.
Prince Saroni's Wife. By JULIAN HAWTHORNE.
The Prince of Wales's Garden-Party. By Mrs. J. H. RIDDELL.
Coals of Fire. By D. CHRISTIE MURRAY. Illustrated by ARTHUR HOPKINS, G. L. SEYMOUR, and D. T. WHITE.
Hearts of Gold. By WILLIAM CYPLES.

Post 8vo, illustrated boards, 2s. each.

Popular Novels, Cheap Editions of.

[WILKIE COLLINS'S NOVELS and BESANT and RICE'S NOVELS may also be had in cloth limp at 2s. 6d. See, too, the PICCADILLY NOVELS, for Library Editions.]

BY EDMOND ABOUT.
The Fellah.

BY HAMILTON AÏDÉ.
Confidences.
Carr of Carrlyon.

BY MRS. ALEXANDER.
Maid, Wife, or Widow?

BY W. BESANT & JAMES RICE.
Ready-Money Mortiboy.
With Harp and Crown.
This Son of Vulcan.
My Little Girl.
The Case of Mr. Lucraft.
The Golden Butterfly.
By Celia's Arbour.
The Monks of Thelema.
'Twas in Trafalgar's Bay.
The Seamy Side.
The Ten Years' Tenant.

BY SHELSLEY BEAUCHAMP.
Grantley Grange.

BY FREDERICK BOYLE.
Camp Notes.
Savage Life.

BY BRET HARTE.
An Heiress of Red Dog.
The Luck of Roaring Camp.
Gabriel Conroy.
Flip.

BY MRS. BURNETT.
Surly Tim.

BY MRS. H. LOVETT CAMERON.
Deceivers Ever.
Juliet's Guardian.

BY MACLAREN COBBAN.
The Cure of Souls.

BY C. ALLSTON COLLINS.
The Bar Sinister.

BY WILKIE COLLINS.
Antonina.
Basil.
Hide and Seek.
The Dead Secret.
The Queen of Hearts.
My Miscellanies.
The Woman in White.
The Moonstone.
Man and Wife.
Poor Miss Finch.
Miss or Mrs.?
The New Magdalen.
The Frozen Deep.
The Law and the Lady.
The Two Destinies.
The Haunted Hotel.
Fallen Leaves.
Jezebel's Daughter.

BY DUTTON COOK.
Leo.

BY MRS. ANNIE EDWARDES.
A Point of Honour.
Archie Lovell.

BY M. BETHAM-EDWARDS.
Felicia.

BY EDWARD EGGLESTON.
Roxy.

BY PERCY FITZGERALD.
Polly.
Bella Donna.
Never Forgotten.
The Second Mrs. Tillotson.
Seventy-five Brooke Street.

BY ALBANY DE FONBLANQUE.
Filthy Lucre.

BY R. E. FRANCILLON.
Olympia.
Queen Cophetua.

BY EDWARD GARRETT.
The Capel Girls.

BY CHARLES GIBBON.
Robin Gray.
For Lack of Gold.
What will the World Say?
In Honour Bound.
The Dead Heart.
In Love and War.
For the King.
Queen of the Meadow.
In Pastures Green.

POPULAR NOVELS—*continued.*

BY *JAMES GREENWOOD.*
Dick Temple.

BY *ANDREW HALLIDAY.*
Every-day Papers.

BY *LADY DUFFUS HARDY.*
Paul Wynter's Sacrifice.

BY *THOMAS HARDY.*
Under the Greenwood Tree.

BY *JULIAN HAWTHORNE.*
Garth.
Ellice Quentin.

BY *TOM HOOD.*
A Golden Heart.

BY *VICTOR HUGO.*
The Hunchback of Notre Dame.

BY *MRS. ALFRED HUNT.*
Thornicroft's Model.

BY *JEAN INGELOW.*
Fated to be Free.

BY *HENRY JAMES, Jun.*
Confidence.

BY *HARRIETT JAY.*
The Queen of Connaught.
The Dark Colleen.

BY *HENRY KINGSLEY.*
Number Seventeen.
Oakshott Castle.

BY *E. LYNN LINTON.*
Patricia Kemball.
Atonement of Leam Dundas.
The World Well Lost.
Under which Lord?
With a Silken Thread.

BY *JUSTIN McCARTHY, M.P.*
The Waterdale Neighbours.
Dear Lady Disdain.
My Enemy's Daughter.
A Fair Saxon.
Linley Rochford.
Miss Misanthrope.
Donna Quixote.

BY *AGNES MACDONELL.*
Quaker Cousins.

BY *KATHARINE S. MACQUOID.*
The Evil Eye.
Lost Rose.

BY *FLORENCE MARRYAT.*
Open! Sesame!
A Harvest of Wild Oats.
A Little Stepson.
Fighting the Air.
Written in Fire.

BY *JEAN MIDDLEMASS.*
Touch and Go.
Mr. Dorillion.

BY *D. CHRISTIE MURRAY.*
A Life's Atonement.

BY *MRS. OLIPHANT.*
Whiteladies.

BY *OUIDA.*
Held in Bondage.
Strathmore.
Chandos.
Under Two Flags.
Idalia.
Cecil Castlemaine's Gage.
Tricotrin.
Puck.
Folle Farine.
A Dog of Flanders.
Pascarel.
Two Little Wooden Shoes.
Signa.
In a Winter City.
Ariadne.
Friendship.
Moths.
Pipistrello.
A Village Commune.

BY *JAMES PAYN.*
Lost Sir Massingberd.
A Perfect Treasure.
Bentinck's Tutor.
Murphy's Master.
A County Family.
At Her Mercy.
A Woman's Vengeance.
Cecil's Tryst.
The Clyffards of Clyffe.
The Family Scapegrace.
The Foster Brothers.
Found Dead.
Gwendoline's Harvest.
Humorous Stories.
Like Father, Like Son.
A Marine Residence.
Married Beneath Him.
Mirk Abbey.

POPULAR NOVELS—*continued.*

JAMES PAYN—*continued.*
Not Wooed, but Won.
Two Hundred Pounds Reward.
The Best of Husbands.
Walter's Word.
Halves.
Fallen Fortunes.
What He Cost Her.
Less Black than we're Painted.
By Proxy.
Under One Roof.
High Spirits.
A Confidential Agent.
Carlyon's Year.

BY EDGAR A. POE.
The Mystery of Marie Roget.

BY CHARLES READE, D.C.L.
It is Never Too Late to Mend.
Hard Cash.
Peg Woffington.
Christie Johnstone.
Griffith Gaunt.
The Double Marriage.
Love Me Little, Love Me Long.
Foul Play.
The Cloister and the Hearth.
The Course of True Love.
The Autobiography of a Thief.
Put Yourself in his Place.

BY MRS. J. H. RIDDELL.
Her Mother's Darling.

BY GEORGE AUGUSTUS SALA.
Gaslight and Daylight.

BY JOHN SAUNDERS.
Bound to the Wheel.
Guy Waterman.
One Against the World.
The Lion in the Path.

BY ARTHUR SKETCHLEY.
A Match in the Dark.

BY WALTER THORNBURY.
Tales for the Marines.

BY ANTHONY TROLLOPE.
The Way we Live Now.
The American Senator.

BY T. ADOLPHUS TROLLOPE.
Diamond Cut Diamond.

BY MARK TWAIN.
A Pleasure Trip in Europe.
Tom Sawyer.
An Idle Excursion.

BY LADY WOOD.
Sabina.

BY EDMUND YATES.
Castaway.
Forlorn Hope.
Land at Last.

ANONYMOUS.
Paul Ferroll.
Why P. Ferroll Killed his Wife.

Fcap. 8vo, picture covers, 1s. each.

Jeff Briggs's Love Story. By BRET HARTE.
The Twins of Table Mountain. By BRET HARTE.
Mrs. Gainsborough's Diamonds. By JULIAN HAWTHORNE.
Kathleen Mavourneen. By the Author of "That Lass o' Lowrie's."
Lindsay's Luck. By the Author of "That Lass o' Lowrie's."
Pretty Polly Pemberton. By the Author of "That Lass o' Lowrie's."
Trooping with Crows. By Mrs. PIRKIS.
The Professor's Wife. By LEONARD GRAHAM.
A Double Bond. By LINDA VILLARI.
Esther's Glove. By R. E. FRANCILLON.
The Garden that Paid the Rent. By TOM JERROLD.

Crown 8vo, cloth extra, with Portrait and Illustrations, 7s. 6d.

Poe's Choice Prose and Poetical Works.

With BAUDELAIRE'S Essay on his Life and Writings.

Planché (J. R.), Works by:

The Cyclopædia of Costume; or, A Dictionary of Dress—Regal, Ecclesiastical, Civil, and Military—from the Earliest Period in England to the Reign of George the Third. Including Notices of Contemporaneous Fashions on the Continent, and a General History of the Costumes of the Principal Countries of Europe. By J. R. PLANCHÉ, Somerset Herald. Two Vols. demy 4to, half morocco, profusely Illustrated with Coloured and Plain Plates and Woodcuts, £7 7s. The Volumes may also be had *separately* (each complete in itself) at £3 13s. 6d. each: Vol. I. THE DICTIONARY. Vol. II. A GENERAL HISTORY OF COSTUME IN EUROPE.

The Pursuivant of Arms; or, Heraldry Founded upon Facts. By J. R. PLANCHÉ. With Coloured Frontispiece and 200 Illustrations. Crown 8vo, cloth extra, 7s. 6d.

Songs and Poems, from 1819 to 1879. By J. R. PLANCHÉ. Edited, with an Introduction, by his Daughter, Mrs. MACKARNESS. Crown 8vo, cloth extra, 6s.

Small 8vo, cloth extra, with 130 Illustrations, 3s. 6d.

Prince of Argolis, The:
A Story of the Old Greek Fairy Time. By J. MOYR SMITH.

Crown 8vo, cloth extra, with Illustrations, 7s. 6d.

Rabelais' Works.
Faithfully Translated from the French, with variorum Notes, and numerous characteristic Illustrations by GUSTAVE DORÉ.

Crown 8vo, cloth gilt, with numerous Illustrations, and a beautifully executed Chart of the various Spectra, 7s. 6d.

Rambosson.—Popular Astronomy.
By J. RAMBOSSON, Laureate of the Institute of France. Translated by C. B. PITMAN. Profusely Illustrated.

Entirely New Edition, Revised, crown 8vo, 1,400 pages, cloth extra, 7s. 6d.

Reader's Handbook (The) of Allusions, References, Plots, and Stories.
By the Rev. Dr. BREWER. Third Edition, revised throughout, with a New Appendix, containing a COMPLETE ENGLISH BIBLIOGRAPHY.

Crown 8vo, cloth extra, 6s.

Richardson. — A Ministry of Health, and other Papers.
By BENJAMIN WARD RICHARDSON, M.D., &c.

Rimmer (Alfred), Works by:

Our Old Country Towns. By ALFRED RIMMER. With over 50 Illustrations by the Author. Square 8vo, cloth extra, gilt, 10s. 6d.

Rambles Round Eton and Harrow. By ALFRED RIMMER. With 50 Illustrations by the Author. Square 8vo, cloth gilt, 10s. 6d. Also an EDITION DE LUXE, in 4to (only a limited number printed), with the Illusts. beautifully printed on China paper, half-bound boards, edges uncut, 42s.

About England with Dickens. With Illustrations by ALFRED RIMMER and C. A. VANDERHOOF. Sq. 8vo, cl. gilt, 10s. 6d. [*In preparation*.

Crown 8vo, cloth extra, 6s.

Robinson.—The Poets' Birds.
By PHIL. ROBINSON, Author of "Noah's Ark," &c. [*In the press*.

Handsomely printed, price 5s.

Roll of Battle Abbey, The;
or, A List of the Principal Warriors who came over from Normandy with William the Conqueror, and Settled in this Country, A.D. 1066-7. With the principal Arms emblazoned in Gold and Colours.

Crown 8vo, cloth extra, profusely Illustrated, 4s. 6d. each.

"Secret Out" Series, The:

The Pyrotechnist's Treasury; or, Complete Art of Making Fireworks. By THOMAS KENTISH. With numerous Illustrations.

The Art of Amusing: A Collection of Graceful Arts, Games, Tricks, Puzzles, and Charades. By FRANK BELLEW. 300 Illustrations.

Hanky-Panky: Very Easy Tricks, Very Difficult Tricks, White Magic, Sleight of Hand. Edited by W. H. CREMER. 200 Illusts.

The Merry Circle: A Book of New Intellectual Games and Amusements. By CLARA BELLEW. Many Illustrations.

Magician's Own Book: Performances with Cups and Balls, Eggs, Hats, Handkerchiefs, &c. All from actual Experience. Edited by W. H. CREMER. 200 Illustrations.

Magic No Mystery: Tricks with Cards, Dice, Balls, &c., with fully descriptive Directions; the Art of Secret Writing; Training of Performing Animals, &c. Coloured Frontispiece and many Illustrations.

The Secret Out: One Thousand Tricks with Cards, and other Recreations; with Entertaining Experiments in Drawing-room or "White Magic." By W. H. CREMER. 300 Engravings.

Crown 8vo, cloth extra, 6s.

Senior.—Travel and Trout in the Antipodes.
An Angler's Sketches in Tasmania and New Zealand. By WILLIAM SENIOR ("Red-Spinner"), Author of "By Stream and Sea."

Shakespeare:

The First Folio Shakespeare.— MR. WILLIAM SHAKESPEARE'S Comedies, Histories, and Tragedies. Published according to the true Originall Copies. London, Printed by ISAAC IAGGARD and ED. BLOUNT. 1623.—A Reproduction of the extremely rare original, in reduced facsimile by a photographic process—ensuring the strictest accuracy in every detail. Small 8vo, half-Roxburghe, 7s. 6d.

The Lansdowne Shakespeare. Beautifully printed in red and black, in small but very clear type. With engraved facsimile of DROESHOUT's Portrait. Post 8vo, cloth extra, 7s. 6d.

Shakespeare for Children: Tales from Shakespeare. By CHARLES and MARY LAMB. With numerous Illustrations, coloured and plain, by J. MOYR SMITH. Crown 4to, cloth gilt, 6s.

The Handbook of Shakespeare Music. Being an Account of 350 Pieces of Music, set to Words taken from the Plays and Poems of Shakespeare, the compositions ranging from the Elizabethan Age to the Present Time. By ALFRED ROFFE. 4to, half-Roxburghe, 7s.

A Study of Shakespeare. By ALGERNON CHARLES SWINBURNE. Crown 8vo, cloth extra, 8s.

Crown 8vo, cloth extra, gilt, with 10 full-page Tinted Illustrations, 7s. 6d.

Sheridan's Complete Works,
with Life and Anecdotes. Including his Dramatic Writings, printed from the Original Editions, his Works in Prose and Poetry, Translations, Speeches, Jokes, Puns, &c. With a Collection of Sheridaniana.

Crown 8vo, cloth extra, with 100 Illustrations, 7s. 6d.
Signboards:
Their History. With Anecdotes of Famous Taverns and Remarkable Characters. By JACOB LARWOOD and JOHN CAMDEN HOTTEN.

Crown 8vo, cloth extra, gilt, 6s. 6d.
Slang Dictionary, The:
Etymological, Historical, and Anecdotal.

Exquisitely printed in miniature, cloth extra, gilt edges, 2s. 6d.
Smoker's Text-Book, The.
By J. HAMER, F.R.S.L.

Demy 8vo, cloth extra, Illustrated, 14s.
South-West, The New:
Travelling Sketches from Kansas, New Mexico, Arizona, and Northern Mexico. By ERNST VON HESSE-WARTEGG. With 100 Fine Illustrations and 3 Maps. [*In preparation*.

Crown 8vo, cloth extra, 5s.
Spalding.—Elizabethan Demonology:
An Essay in Illustration of the Belief in the Existence of Devils, and the Powers possessed by them. By T. ALFRED SPALDING, LL.B.

Crown 4to, with Coloured Illustrations, cloth gilt, 6s.
Spenser for Children.
By M. H. TOWRY. With Illustrations by WALTER J. MORGAN.

A New Edition, small crown 8vo, cloth extra, 5s.
Staunton.—Laws and Practice of Chess;
Together with an Analysis of the Openings, and a Treatise on End Games. By HOWARD STAUNTON. Edited by ROBERT B. WORMALD.

Crown 8vo, cloth extra, 9s.
Stedman.—Victorian Poets:
Critical Essays. By EDMUND CLARENCE STEDMAN.

Stevenson (R. Louis), Works by:
Familiar Studies of Men and Books. By R. LOUIS STEVENSON. Crown 8vo, cloth extra, 6s.
New Arabian Nights. By R. LOUIS STEVENSON. Two Vols. post 8vo, 12s.
"*We must place the 'New Arabian Nights' very high indeed, almost hors concours, among the fiction of the present day.*"—PALL MALL GAZETTE.

Two Vols., crown 8vo, with numerous Portraits and Illustrations, 24s.
Strahan.—Twenty Years of a Publisher's
Life. By ALEXANDER STRAHAN. [*In preparation*

Crown 8vo, cloth extra, with Illustrations, 7s. 6d.
Strutt's Sports and Pastimes of the People of
England; including the Rural and Domestic Recreations, May Games, Mummeries, Shows, Processions, Pageants, and Pompous Spectacles, from the Earliest Period to the Present Time. With 140 Illustrations. Edited by WILLIAM HONE.

Crown 8vo, with a Map of Suburban London, cloth extra, 7s. 6d.
Suburban Homes (The) of London:
A Residential Guide to Favourite London Localities, their Society, Celebrities, and Associations. With Notes on their Rental, Rates, and House Accommodation.

Crown 8vo, cloth extra, with Illustrations, 7s. 6d.
Swift's Choice Works,
In Prose and Verse. With Memoir, Portrait, and Facsimiles of the Maps in the Original Edition of "Gulliver's Travels."

Swinburne's (Algernon C.) Works:

The Queen Mother and Rosamond. Fcap. 8vo, 5s.

Atalanta in Calydon.
A New Edition. Crown 8vo, 6s.

Chastelard.
A Tragedy. Crown 8vo, 7s.

Poems and Ballads.
FIRST SERIES. Fcap. 8vo, 9s. Also in crown 8vo, at same price.

Poems and Ballads.
SECOND SERIES. Fcap. 8vo, 9s. Also in crown 8vo, at same price.

Notes on Poems and Reviews.
8vo, 1s.

William Blake:
A Critical Essay. With Facsimile Paintings. Demy 8vo, 16s.

Songs before Sunrise.
Crown 8vo, 10s. 6d.

Bothwell:
A Tragedy. Crown 8vo, 12s. 6d.

George Chapman:
An Essay. Crown 8vo, 7s.

Songs of Two Nations.
Crown 8vo, 6s.

Essays and Studies.
Crown 8vo, 12s.

Erechtheus:
A Tragedy. Crown 8vo, 6s.

Note of an English Republican on the Muscovite Crusade. 8vo, 1s.

A Note on Charlotte Bronte.
Crown 8vo, 6s.

A Study of Shakespeare.
Crown 8vo, 8s.

Songs of the Springtides.
Crown 8vo, 6s.

Studies in Song.
Crown 8vo, 7s.

Mary Stuart:
A Tragedy. Crown 8vo, 8s.

Tristram of Lyonesse, and other Poems. Crown 8vo, 9s.

Medium 8vo, cloth extra, with Illustrations, 7s. 6d.
Syntax's (Dr.) Three Tours,
In Search of the Picturesque, in Search of Consolation, and in Search of a Wife. With the whole of ROWLANDSON'S droll page Illustrations in Colours, and a Life of the Author by J. C. HOTTEN.

Four Vols. small 8vo, cloth boards, 30s.
Taine's History of English Literature.
Translated by HENRY VAN LAUN.

₊ Also a POPULAR EDITION, in Two Vols. crown 8vo, cloth extra, 15s.

Crown 8vo, cloth gilt, profusely Illustrated, 6s.
Tales of Old Thule.
Collected and Illustrated by J. MOYR SMITH.

One Vol., crown 8vo, cloth extra, 7s. 6d.
Taylor's (Tom) Historical Dramas:
"Clancarty," "Jeanne Darc," "'Twixt Axe and Crown," "The Fool's Revenge," "Arkwright's Wife," "Anne Boleyn," "Plot and Passion."
*_** The Plays may also be had separately, at 1s. each.

Crown 8vo, cloth extra, with numerous Illustrations, 7s. 6d.
Thackerayana:
Notes and Anecdotes. Illustrated by a profusion of Sketches by WILLIAM MAKEPEACE THACKERAY, depicting Humorous Incidents in his School-life, and Favourite Characters in the books of his every-day reading. With Coloured Frontispiece and Hundreds of Wood Engravings, facsimiled from Mr. Thackeray's Original Drawings.

Crown 8vo, cloth extra, gilt edges, with Illustrations, 7s. 6d.
Thomson's Seasons and Castle of Indolence.
With a Biographical and Critical Introduction by ALLAN CUNNINGHAM, and over 50 fine Illustrations on Steel and Wood.

Thornbury (Walter), Works by:
Haunted London. By WALTER THORNBURY. A New Edition, Edited by EDWARD WALFORD, M.A., with numerous Illustrations by F. W. FAIRHOLT, F.S.A. Crown 8vo, cloth extra, 7s. 6d.

The Life and Correspondence of J. M. W. Turner. Founded upon Letters and Papers furnished by his Friends and fellow Academicians. By WALTER THORNBURY. A New Edition, considerably Enlarged. With numerous Illustrations in Colours, facsimiled from Turner's Original Drawings. Crown 8vo, cloth extra, 7s. 6d.

Timbs (John), Works by:
Clubs and Club Life in London. With Anecdotes of its Famous Coffee-houses, Hostelries, and Taverns. By JOHN TIMBS, F.S.A. With numerous Illustrations. Crown 8vo, cloth extra, 7s. 6d.

English Eccentrics and Eccentricities: Stories of Wealth and Fashion, Delusions, Impostures, and Fanatic Missions, Strange Sights and Sporting Scenes, Eccentric Artists, Theatrical Folks, Men of Letters, &c. By JOHN TIMBS, F.S.A. With nearly 50 Illustrations. Crown 8vo, cloth extra, 7s. 6d.

Demy 8vo, cloth extra, 14s.
Torrens.—The Marquess Wellesley,
Architect of Empire. An Historic Portrait. *Forming Vol. I. of* PROCONSUL and TRIBUNE: WELLESLEY and O'CONNELL: Historic Portraits. By W. M. TORRENS, M.P. In Two Vols.

Two Vols., crown 8vo, cloth extra, with Map and Ground-Plans, 14s.
Walcott.—Church Work and Life in English
Minsters; and the English Student's Monasticon. By the Rev. MACKENZIE E. C. WALCOTT, B.D.

The Twenty-third Annual Edition, for 1883, cloth, full gilt, 50s.

Walford.—The County Families of the United Kingdom.

By EDWARD WALFORD, M.A. Containing Notices of the Descent, Birth, Marriage, Education, &c., of more than 12,000 distinguished Heads of Families, their Heirs Apparent or Presumptive, the Offices they hold or have held, their Town and Country Addresses, Clubs, &c. [*In the press.*

Large crown 8vo, cloth antique, with Illustrations, 7s. 6d.

Walton and Cotton's Complete Angler;

or, The Contemplative Man's Recreation; being a Discourse of Rivers, Fishponds, Fish and Fishing, written by IZAAK WALTON; and Instructions how to Angle for a Trout or Grayling in a clear Stream, by CHARLES COTTON. With Original Memoirs and Notes by Sir HARRIS NICOLAS, and 61 Copperplate Illustrations.

Crown 8vo, cloth extra, 3s. 6d. per volume.

Wanderer's Library, The:

Merrie England in the Olden Time. By GEORGE DANIEL. With Illustrations by ROBT. CRUIKSHANK.

The Old Showmen and the Old London Fairs. By THOMAS FROST.

The Wilds of London. By JAMES GREENWOOD.

Tavern Anecdotes and Sayings; Including the Origin of Signs, and Reminiscences connected with Taverns, Coffee Houses, Clubs, &c. By CHARLES HINDLEY. With Illusts.

Circus Life and Circus Celebrities. By THOMAS FROST.

The Lives of the Conjurers. By THOMAS FROST.

The Life and Adventures of a Cheap Jack. By One of the Fraternity. Edited by CHARLES HINDLEY.

The Story of the London Parks. By JACOB LARWOOD. With Illusts.

Low-Life Deeps. An Account of the Strange Fish to be found there. By JAMES GREENWOOD.

Seven Generations of Executioners: Memoirs of the Sanson Family (1688 to 1847). Edited by HENRY SANSON.

The World Behind the Scenes. By PERCY FITZGERALD.

London Characters. By HENRY MAYHEW. Illustrated.

The Genial Showman: Life and Adventures of Artemus Ward. By E. P. HINGSTON. Frontispiece.

Wanderings in Patagonia; or, Life among the Ostrich Hunters. By JULIUS BEERBOHM. Illustrated.

Summer Cruising in the South Seas. By CHARLES WARREN STODDARD. Illust. by WALLIS MACKAY.

Savage Life. By FREDERICK BOYLE.

Camp Notes: Stories of Sport and Adventure in Asia, Africa, and America. By FREDERICK BOYLE.

Tunis: The Land and the People. By the Chevalier de HESSE-WARTEGG. With 22 Illustrations.

Carefully printed on paper to imitate the Original, 22 in. by 14 in., 2s.

Warrant to Execute Charles I.

An exact Facsimile of this important Document, with the Fifty-nine Signatures of the Regicides, and corresponding Seals.

Beautifully printed on paper to imitate the Original MS., price 2s.

Warrant to Execute Mary Queen of Scots.

An exact Facsimile, including the Signature of Queen Elizabeth, and a Facsimile of the Great Seal.

Crown 8vo, cloth limp, with numerous Illustrations, 4s. 6d.

Westropp.—Handbook of Pottery and Porcelain; or, History of those Arts from the Earliest Period. By HODDER M. WESTROPP. With numerous Illustrations, and a List of Marks.

SEVENTH EDITION. Square 8vo, 1s.

Whistler v. Ruskin: Art and Art Critics.
By J. A. MACNEILL WHISTLER.

Williams (Mattieu), Works by:
Science in Short Chapters. By W. MATTIEU WILLIAMS, F.R.A.S., F.C.S. Crown 8vo, cloth extra, 7s. 6d.
A Simple Treatise on Heat. By W. MATTIEU WILLIAMS F.R.A.S., F.C.S. Crown 8vo, cloth limp, with Illustrations, 2s. 6d.

Wilson (Dr. Andrew), Works by:
Chapters on Evolution: A Popular History of the Darwinian and Allied Theories of Development. By ANDREW WILSON, Ph.D., F.R.S.E. Crown 8vo, cloth extra, with 259 Illustrations, 7s. 6d.
Leaves from a Naturalist's Note-book. By ANDREW WILSON, Ph.D., F.R.S.E. (A Volume of "The Mayfair Library.") Post 8vo, cloth limp, 2s. 6d.
Leisure-Time Studies, chiefly Biological. By ANDREW WILSON, Ph.D., F.R.S.E. Second Edition. Crown 8vo, cloth extra, with Illustrations, 6s.

"*It is well when we can take up the work of a really qualified investigator, who in the intervals of his more serious professional labours sets himself to impart knowledge in such a simple and elementary form as may attract and instruct, with no danger of misleading the tyro in natural science. Such a work is this little volume, made up of essays and addresses written and delivered by Dr. Andrew Wilson, lecturer and examiner in Science at Edinburgh and Glasgow, at leisure intervals in a busy professional life. . . . Dr. Wilson's pages teem with matter stimulating to a healthy love of science and a reverence for the truths of nature.*"—SATURDAY REVIEW.

Small 8vo, cloth extra, Illustrated, 6s.

Wooing (The) of the Water Witch:
A Northern Oddity. By EVAN DALDORNE. Illust. by J. MOYR SMITH.

Crown 8vo, half-bound, 12s. 6d.

Words, Facts, and Phrases:
A Dictionary of Curious, Quaint, and Out-of-the-Way Matters. By ELIEZER EDWARDS.

Wright (Thomas), Works by:
Caricature History of the Georges. (The House of Hanover.) With 400 Pictures, Caricatures, Squibs, Broadsides, Window Pictures, &c. By THOMAS WRIGHT, F.S.A. Crown 8vo, cloth extra, 7s. 6d.
History of Caricature and of the Grotesque in Art, Literature, Sculpture, and Painting. By THOMAS WRIGHT, F.S.A. Profusely Illustrated by F. W. FAIRHOLT, F.S.A. Large post 8vo, cloth extra, 7s. 6d.

J. OGDEN AND CO., PRINTERS, 172, ST. JOHN STREET, E.C.

www.ingramcontent.com/pod-product-compliance
Lightning Source LLC
Chambersburg PA
CBHW030357170426
43202CB00010B/1399